Chaver Up!

49 Rabbis Explore What it Means to be an Ally through a Jewish Lens

Rabbi Sharon Kleinbaum &
Rabbi Mike Moskowitz
(Editors)

Beit Simchat Torah CONGREGATION

קהלה קדושה בית שמחת תורה

Table of Contents

Introduction

Rabbis Sharon Kleinbaum and
Mike Moskowitz

What does it mean to be an ally?

Ally, as a noun, has evolved in meaning from a person or state who helps another to a more pointed kind of social/political advocacy. As David M. Hall writes in the Merriam/Webster dictionary, it is often now used to describe "a person who is not a member of a marginalized or mistreated group but who expresses or gives support to that group. . . allies are people who support LGBT rights but aren't LGBT themselves."

Currently, we understand an ally to be someone in a position of privilege who chooses to act on behalf of others who are more at risk.

Of course, many of us are at risk in one aspect of life and yet are also able to be an ally to others. It is important to realize this, lest we fall into the misguided binary of assuming that the one at risk is a victim, and the one helping is condescending and/or powerful. When we see ourselves as simultaneously needing allies and as capable of being allies, we are most aligned with the Divine plan. We are living in holy space when we can *act* with the power of allyship and also *receive* the gift of allyship.

Mishnah Avot 6:6 teaches that in order to acquire Torah, one must be נוֹשֵׂא בְעֹל עִם חֲבֵרוֹ, sharing in the burden of one's friend (Chaver). The Maharal of Prague explains that if the Mishna wanted us to simply support others in their struggle, then the Mishnah would have written "נוֹשֵׂא עִם חֲבֵרוֹ בְּעֹל" to share the burden with our friends. By requiring us to *share in the burden of one's friend*, the Mishnah is asking us to personally take on the burden and relieve the one being pressed down by it.

נוֹשֵׂא בְּעֹל עִם חֲבֵרוֹ is listed, by the Maharal, as the last of the 48 ways that the Mishnah teaches that Torah can be acquired. This indicates that it is the culmination of the previous 47. It is not simple to be an ally. It requires a lot of thoughtful preparation and a deep sense of communal responsibility.

The Torah is also called an "עוֹל," a load meant to be carried. We are coming together as rabbis, as teachers, to ally with the Torah to give it voice and to carry it. The Midrash in Vayikra Rabbah 1:3 explains that one of Moses' names is "Chaver/Ally" because he allied the people of Israel with G-d.

Discrimination encourages people to think of themselves as being distinct from those being oppressed. Learning about the lives, struggles, and needs of people suffering from inequality is necessary in forming our role as part of the solution. It is also essential to feel so much a part of the whole, that the needs of another are one's own. Our common humanity, connecting us through the Divine Image, is much greater than any perceived difference.

Although this is a truth that we must live every day, we have chosen this time of the Hebrew

2

calendar, the counting of the 49 days of the Omer, to publish these teachings from 49 spiritual leaders as diverse as our people. In this time between Passover and Shavuot, the Israelites came together to receive the Torah at Mount Sinai. Sadly later in our history, during the same 49 days of the Omer, 24,000 students of Rebbe Akiva died because they did not afford each other the proper dignity. We hope that this collection of essays will both celebrate our unity and encourage us to recognize the essential dignity of each person. By banding together as allies, we can strive to re-experience the moment that we all stood together at Sinai.

But how to be an ally? And in what ways have each of our lives been transformed by acts of allyship of others? These are the questions at the heart of this collection of essays. Allyship is hard work and many mistakes get made. We know though, when we struggle on the path of allyship, we are struggling on the path of G-d.

Taking Action (and Responsibility)

Rabbi Rachel Barenblat

Allyship means placing myself in the shoes of someone experiencing marginalization or oppression, "taking on their struggle as my own," recognizing where and how today's structures give me privilege that they don't have, and trying to transfer the benefits of my privilege to them.[1] Allyship asks me to be active in standing up for those who are oppressed or marginalized. And allyship asks me, when I inevitably err, to take responsibility, to apologize, and to learn better and try better next time.

One way to understand allyship is through a Mussar lens. Mussar is a Jewish practice of self-refinement through focusing on and developing our *middot* or soul-qualities. When I think of allyship, the middah that comes to mind is *achrayut*, "responsibility." The term is related to the word *achar*, "after." We need to pay attention to what happens after we act (or refrain from action). If I ignore injustice or power disparity because I'm not the person being harmed, what happens after? If I speak or act (or fail to speak or act) in a way that causes harm, what happens

---

1 Lamont, Amelie (n.d) *The Guide to Allyship*. Available from https://guidetoallyship.com/ (accessed February 17, 2021).

after? Achrayut reminds us of our ethical obligation to keep impacts and outcomes in mind.

But put a different vowel in that word, and achar becomes *acher*, "other." That suggests another, equally important, implication of *achrayut*. When we care for each other, we express and strengthen our *achrayut*. *Achrayut* means actively taking the responsibility of caring for another, or an "other." *Achrayut* means centering the needs of the other. Unlike the term "allyship," *achrayut* doesn't presume a power differential between the person with needs and the person with privilege who's centering those needs. Still, the *middah* of *achrayut* can fuel our allyship.

Some dislike the language of allyship, because it can maintain a distance between the person with power and the person who is marginalized or oppressed. Good intentions are not enough, and keeping "their" problems at arm's-length is not enough. As Roxanne Gay writes:[2]

> Black people do not need allies. We need people to stand up and take on the problems borne of oppression as their own, without remove or distance. We need people to do this even if they cannot fully understand what it's like to be oppressed

---

2 Gay, Roxanne, 2016. "On Making Black Lives Matter." *Marie Claire* (June 11). Available from https://www.marieclaire.com/culture/a21423/roxane-gay-philando-castile-alton-sterling/ (accessed February 5, 2021).

for their race or ethnicity, gender, sexuality, ability, class, religion, or other marker of identity.

Black people need those of us who are white to stand up and take on the problems borne of oppression as our own. Queer people need those of us who are straight to do likewise. Trans* people need those of us who are cisgender to do likewise. And so on. "Stand up" and "take on" are active verbs. Allyship must be more than platitudes: it asks action. So too does the Torah.

In Deuteronomy (22.8) we find the commandment to put a guardrail or parapet upon our roofs, lest someone fall from the roof of the home we inhabit and thereby be harmed. G-d commands us to take action as we take responsibility for the needs of the other. The Talmud (Shabbat 45b) takes that mitzvah even further: if we could prevent someone in our household from causing harm, we are obligated to do so. If we can prevent anyone in the world from causing harm, we are obligated to do that, too! Because if we could prevent harm and we don't do so, we become responsible for the outcome. This, too, is part of allyship for me.

The actions of allyship, building relationships with those who are marginalized or oppressed, accompanying them, standing up for them, centering their needs and amplifying their voices, sharing with them the benefits of unearned privilege, are an extension of this mitzvah. It's incumbent on all of us to make sure that our "houses" are safe, and that no one will experience harm from "falling off our roof." Which is to say, we need to ensure that our relational and communal spaces are safe for everyone, that those who lack privilege are lifted up into privilege, and that no one will experience harm from structures of privilege and power. That's the work. We may not be able to complete it, but we're obligated to do what we can.

The Mitzvah of Allyship

Rabbi Rick Jacobs

Being Jewish is at the core of who I am, and for most of my life, I have moved safely through Jewish spaces without feeling the need for an ally. I am a straight, cisgender, white Ashkenazi Jewish man, living without a disability, who is a rabbi, a baby boomer, and the child of two Jewish parents. While I've both witnessed and personally experienced antisemitism, my dominant identities have granted me access to most spaces, and I have found nearly every Jewish door open to me along my life's journey.

But in recent years, I've spoken with individuals from many marginalized backgrounds whose experiences in Jewish spaces have been more difficult than my own. They made it abundantly clear that more often than not, people failed to acknowledge, disrupt, and prevent these harmful and othering experiences. I had to ask myself, "Where was I in those moments? How do I say, *Hineini,* here I am, to those who count on me to build more inclusive and equitable Jewish communities? How can I be the ally that I personally never needed?"

Yolanda Savage-Narva, the Union for Reform Judaism's director of racial equity, diversity, and inclusion (and one of my teachers), teaches that "ally" is a verb, not a noun. To ally is not simply to offer support and encouragement to those on the margins. It requires the courage to disrupt a problematic moment, to acknowledge who's missing from a conversation, planning committee, or leadership team. Allyship is far from simple; it takes a lot of practice and the bravery to allow oneself to make mistakes and to be accountable for them.

To ally means to embody the spirit of Moshe Rabeinu (Moses our Teacher), who witnessed shepherds driving off the seven daughters of the Midianite priest who were trying to water their father's flock. Instead of shying away because it was someone else's problem, or because these women belonged to a different faith community, Moses "rose to their defense" (Exodus 2:17). In that moment, he didn't see the distinction between Jew and Midianite; he saw men harassing women and he stepped in. He allied because it was the right thing to do.

If Moses experienced a similar encounter with these women today, I imagine he should ask them, "How do you need me to act? Do I step forward on your behalf? Do I stand nearby while you assert your right to draw from the well?" As Jewish leaders, if we seek to emulate our greatest teacher, we should not assume that allying always means leading up front. Those of us with many privileges and opportunities need to lead in the way we're needed in each moment, and at times, that means stepping back and supporting those who need it. And yet, it is often hard to know the most respectful way to ally in such situations.

At the URJ, we have been working hard to learn how to most effectively ally and inspire others to take on this sacred work. For example, one way I express allyship is through sharing my pronouns whenever I introduce myself. Doing so is one of many ways we can foster loving, respectful, and diverse communities in regard to gender identity. And yet, for some who are not familiar with this spiritual practice, when it's their turn to share their pronouns, they become flustered or even dismissive. In moments like this, I ally by calmly reminding them what's at stake. Suicide and hate crimes are a significant cause of death for transgender and nonbinary people, and something as simple as sharing our pronouns (and honoring others' pronouns) can literally help save lives. Affirming the sanctity of the variety of pronouns we use can make the difference between death and the loving embrace of real community.

It's been six years since the first of our fifteen overnight summer camps welcomed Hannah, our first transgender camper. Our entire camp community, campers, parents, clergy, staff, allied with Hannah through the sacred act of learning. Louis Bordman, then the director of URJ Eisner Camp in Great Barrington, MA, led a large-scale community-wide education so that this camp would be a true home to Hannah and others like her. Louis communicated: "Hannah had previously attended camp as a boy. At age 11, Hannah's family approached us asking if we would welcome her at camp that summer as she transitioned socially to a girl. That began a process designed to enable us to say, yes, Hannah would be welcome at URJ Eisner Camp, just like other girls her age." Allyship meant engaging in a careful, intentional process that not only made Hannah's beloved summer camp a place where she could safely be herself, but that also educated and empowered that camp community to better embrace trans campers, staff, parents, and community members in the future.

This reflective experience gave us the confidence to more explicitly fight for trans inclusion at our 2015 URJ Biennial convention. Our Resolution on the Rights of Transgender and Gender Non-Conforming People was one of the most far-reaching statements by a religious movement in recent history, and our 5,000 delegates from all over North America voted unanimously in favor of it. While that moment was a critical affirmation of our Movement's commitment, the real work is in living up to the resolution's commitments. I return again to Yolanda's teaching: "ally" is a verb, not a noun; this mitzvah requires action in the crucible of challenging moments. The instances when we least want to stand up and ally are often the ones when we most need to.

As Jews, we cannot claim to follow our divine imperative of pursuing justice until we acknowledge that inequities exist both outside and within our communities. Fighting societal injustice is inauthentic without addressing the daily micro- and macro-aggressive racial abuses that Jews of Color endure in our communities. To ally means to speak up when these abuses are witnessed, not to "sit idly by." Will doing so sometimes cause discomfort? Of course it will. I've certainly felt uncomfortable when I've been "called in" for unintentionally saying or doing something insensitive: and yet, those moments were blessings because they served as learning experiences. Receiving rebuke, whether offered lovingly or harshly, is a skill those of us who are used to being at the microphone of Jewish life must embrace.

To ally also requires learning and collaboration. In writing this piece and most others, I consult with wise colleagues at the URJ who lead our Audacious Hospitality work. Yolanda Savage-Narva, Chris Harrison, Rachel Hall, and Jaimie Green all helped inform and sharpen my thoughts in this piece and at large. I can safely say that mentors who challenge and inspire you are essential to becoming the ally your communities need you to be.

Twelfth-century Torah commentator Ibn Ezra offers a moving comment on Deuteronomy 27:19, which includes a curse for those who "subvert the rights of the stranger, the orphan, and the widow." His comment suggests that each of these individuals makes their way through the world without allies, thus making their lives immeasurably more painful and challenging. While the terms stranger, orphan, and widow are certainly archaic terms today, Ibn Ezra's commentary on advocating and allying with those on the margins is timeless. I pray that we will all work together to ally in the ways that our communities' members need, to create a Jewish landscape rooted in diversity, equity, and inclusion where, G-d willing, the mitzvah of allyship will one day no longer be needed.

This work begins with each of us. What are we waiting for?

Parenting and Allyship

Rabbi Ari Poster Moffic

When I think about who I am, it's impossible to tell my story without focusing on my children. They are inextricably part of how I understand my role in life, my daily pursuits and my worldview. Their interests are now part of my knowledge base, even if I would not have been drawn to these areas independently. Their needs are my obsession. I am their advocate. I am their helper. I am their guide, protector and provider along with my husband. Other people play vital roles, of course, in their lives, but we are primary.

People come into our lives and we are changed by the encounter. Our oldest was born with a host of medical conditions that became apparent in the first few years of her life. They impacted bodily functions and took over the rhythm of our days. They involved numerous appointments, tests, procedures, and medicines. Everyone who knew her had an opinion about her condition. I felt judged. I felt inadequate. Today, I am in Facebook groups with other parents who have children with her illness and feel myself to be an expert on how to help her navigate life, while always learning new things. I had never heard of her condition before she was born. Now, I am her ally. I stand with her. I speak with her and for her at times. We celebrate when we find a good treatment or get through a hard situation together. I don't know exactly what it's like to have the medical issues she deals with. However, I have an up-close, extremely personal, raw, real, tactile experience of it. I am her ally because I want the medical community to grow in empathy and understanding, and it will take parents from this community to work together to make this happen. In this case, I am associated with and connected to this medical cause with a certain goal in mind of cure and knowledge.

Then came our youngest. It turns out she is transgender. It turns out she has lots of other initials as part of her bio. And the allyship journey started all over again for her, with her, and because of her. Learning, growing, asking, putting ourselves out there for spectacle, judgement and even praise.

Allyship is about me in relationship with them. It's about my experience as a parent to two children with issues that require advocacy in order to make the world a better, more understanding and safer place. I am an ally because the children I stand with are growing up with conditions and experiences that require them to be unduly strong, brave, courageous, stoic, and vulnerable. I wouldn't say that being an ally is easy and being in a vulnerable population is hard. These are false binaries.

Sometimes people in their communities, with their identities and conditions, tell me I am not part of their group. I am not one of them. I can't speak for them or on their behalf unless directly asked. I am a cis, straight, neurotypical person who is peripheral and adjacent. Who is in? Who is out? How can an ally stay in their lane and still be effective? When we are at the doctor or in public, I need to be their friend, partner, and helper, all the terms associated with being an ally. But, do I need to call myself that? To add that to *my* identity? To dare to think that makes me closer to the groups my children are in? I can be their ally while knowing the people in their cohorts will lead the way. In Genesis we read, "Isaac could not make out Jacob's identity because his hands were hairy, as were those of his brother Esau; and he decided to bless him."

I have not taken on the identity of my children. I am similar though. They have changed me. They have rubbed off on me. I am not pretending to be them.

There is no ally like a parent. But Isaac could have been an ally to both.

"Show Me Your Way": The Trans Microcosm of Spiritual Allyship

Rabbi David Evan Markus

"Andy" sent a spiritual autobiography of four pages, a shimmeringly honest reflection on Andy's emotional and spiritual life; birth family and chosen family, loves and losses, belief and disbelief, hope and yearning. Its treatment of gender identity spanned 10 pivotal words: "I'm trans of [*gender*] experience and completed transition some years ago."

I sat in *yir'ah* (awe), partly that Andy gifted me the trust of coming out to me at all; an unknown cisgendered straight male becoming their new spiritual director. Mostly my awe was that Andy articulated their trans experience as one of many facets shining, sometimes brightly, sometimes darkly, on and through Andy's spiritual life.

I said to myself, "Andy, show me your way because I have a lot to learn."

Andy would be among my first spiritual directees of trans experience and, thankfully, far from the last. Every trans seeker who shared spiritual intimacy in our shared sacred journey has taught me about G-d, Judaism and especially allyship.

We agreed to ditch the title "spiritual direction," which falsely implies that I'm a "director" who "directs" something, and that what I "direct" is "spiritual:" as if authentic spirituality were directable by human agency, much less mine. Rather than this term's implied egotism and verticality, I prefer the Hebrew term *hashpa'ah*, which uplifts the allyship and sacred art of seeking, witnessing and priming *shefa* (sacred flow) through the whole of one's life experience. Befitting that posture, *hashpa'ah* channels awe and open curiosity at the revelation unfolding in each unique soul's encounter with each day.

My "directees" of trans experience illustrate how.

The De-Essentialization of Trans Spirituality

Dr. Rachel Mann, a theologian of trans experience, observed in her "Queering Spiritual Direction" that traditional spiritual direction notions (and many other faith-based structures and practices) alienate people of trans experience in ways glaringly visible to them, but often obscure if not invisible to would-be allies. Orthodoxies of thought, belief and language reflect and reinforce spiritual normativities based on seemingly immutable gendered constructs. In response, even without the coercion of divine "gender" and societal moralisms around "conforming" gender identity, generations of trans seekers have felt overwhelming pressure, sometimes with violent physical, psychic and moral force, to conform or rebel at profound cost to body, heart and soul.

It is little wonder that Dr. Laura Thor, who pioneered spiritual direction's evolution toward wiser allyship for persons of trans experience, noted that in trans contexts, spiritual accompaniment asks heightened awareness of trans experiences of internal and external alienation. She urges that clergy and other spiritual accompanists cannot be true trans allies without appreciating prevalent spiritual, emotional and political facets of that experience, because trans experience is perhaps second to none in its collective history of invisibility, prejudice, repression and forced reformation. As Thor writes:

> Transgender spiritual directees are profoundly marginalized hidden seekers of G-d and their spiritual birthright to simply live as they are intended. Many who come out are ejected from their religious communities; others live in secrecy and are unable to locate themselves in Creation.

These kinds of observations, earned by decades of hard-won experience inside and alongside the trans community, point cisgendered allies toward what we can know and, as importantly, what we can't. While cisgendered allies might wish to believe that empathy can cultivate understanding of trans experience, we lack the intuition that only identification and experience can cultivate. Allyship means knowing just that: what we can't fully know and, indeed, what isn't ours to fully know.

Yet too often, well-intended "woke" allies peer into trans experience from outside and infer what we can't intuit. They essentialize trans experience, imputing stereotypes and other characteristics they believe are inherent or "essential." An essentializing eye often fails to see individuals fully for who they are and who they're becoming. Who with a history of feeling unseen will welcome feeling unseen again, especially by would-be allies and so-called helpers? Thus, allies who hew to *any* transgender spiritual prototype, essentializing trans spirituality to be a given way, can cause harm no less dispiriting than ones who look past (or go blind to) prevalent trans experience. Spiritual leaders especially risk these harms because of the higher stakes in spiritual contexts. And because *hashpa'ah* cultivates exquisite trust with open hearts and rightfully high expectations of safety, essentialization in a *hashpa'ah* context can trigger especially deep pain. Particularly in these tender places, spiritual allies must make every effort to banish essentialization from their hearts and minds.

Mutuality, Awesome Encounter and Skillful Means

How can cisgendered allies spiritually companion people of trans experience? I preface first responses by underscoring that answers are not mainly for would-be allies like me to offer.

Much as each heart knows its own landscape and especially its own bitterness (Proverbs 14:10), each soul knows its own yearning, joys and oys. Especially for anyone who has felt unseen or worse, the parameters of principled discernment for spiritual encounter must be empowering and mutual. Wise allies will explicitly narrate this first principle from the start and completely honor it.

To be sure, this first principle applies to all spiritual accompaniment: for the cisgendered straight, the lesbian, the gay, the bisexual, the asexual, the gender nonconforming, the queer, the questioning and the one who does not yet know to ask. Thus, the trans seeker exemplifies a general principle that always finds a particular expression for each seeker with their unique history and context.

This first principle implies a second in which a trans seeker offers a microcosmic reminder of spiritual experience generally. The de-essentialization of trans spirituality demands that allies approach and support spiritual encounters in a radical posture of awe: not "as if" in the sacred presence of transcendent revelation but precisely "in" the sacred presence of transcendent revelation. As Jewish queer theory scholars Dr. Caryn Aviv and Dr. Karen Erlichman observed, the *lech lecha* of G-d's first deployment for Avram (Genesis 12:1) is best translated not as "Go out" but "Go to yourself," so each of us inhabits a landscape of spiritual, gender and sexual revelation *asher ar'eka* ("that [G-d] will show [us]"). As the Psalmist put it, we ourselves are spiritual revelations unfolding each at our own sacred pace: "Here I am, coming with sacred writing on me ... Your guidance [revealed as] my innermost part" (Psalm 40:8-9). It follows that most everything in our lives, including pathways of trans life, can be paths by which we might seek and experience divinity: "Know G-d in *all* your ways" (Proverbs 3:6).

This unfolding reflects divine becoming itself. In Rabbi Mike Moskowitz's words, Torah records the sacred "I am," the first of the Ten Commandments (Exodus 20:2, Deuteronomy 5:6), as G-d's self-revelation, a "coming out" that continuously models liberating authenticity. If so, then essentialization has no rightful place, especially in the presence of *HaMakom*, the omni-Presence we feebly call G-d. Here again, trans seekers can teach allies a key lesson applicable to all.

At the same time, the de-essentialization of trans spirituality challenges allies not to lose the forest for the proverbial trees. Even as we honor spiritual individuality, the trans community's collective experience can suggest much about any one individual's personal experience, whether one's own experience literally or in association with the community. How many times has Biblical moralism impressed on trans seekers a G-d assigned a gender? Or recorded to create each person with an immutable gender? Or heard to ban cross-dressing, much less same-sex intimacy? How many times have religious and other societal forces wielded spiritual authority by telling people of trans experience that they and their lives are deluded, defective or immoral? How many were left feeling that G-d betrayed them? How many turned away from G-d? How many risked or lost families, livelihoods and lives by coming out? How could these personal and collective experiences not shape spiritual belief, identity and intimacy?

And more affirmatively, how many people of trans experience found courage, resilience, empowerment, truth, liberation, community, love, grace, meaning and whole new ways of spirit in their gender identity journeys? How many learned to seek and find the sacred in lives they once felt were anything but sacred? How many redeemed their suffering to learn, in Dr. Victor Frankl's words, that what gives light must endure burning? How many became beacons for others because their own light shined bright?

An ally unaware of these communal dynamics cannot be most effective, but neither can an ally who essentializes spirituality by imposing these prevalent dynamics as stereotypes, however well intentioned. If it sounds like a brain-teasing koan, like the sound of one hand clapping, maybe it is.

To me, this koan asks allies to cultivate the same open curiosity and radical awe at each soul's sacred revelation unfolding in each moment. At the same time, it asks allies to cultivate peripheral awareness of the collective wisdom gleaned by decades of experience inside and alongside the trans community, and to hold that peripheral awareness without putting any of it on anyone.

Andy showed how a spiritual journey can be both individually unique and also reflective of prevalent community experience. Andy experienced patterns of distrust, anger, self-doubt and spiritual guarding that came to weigh on their heart. Andy hadn't considered that the sacred might manifest in that awareness and what it might teach when Andy decided they were ready. Self-doubt and self-loathing revealed patterns Andy took on and believed they'd outgrown after they transitioned. Spiritual guarding opened into courage to express their sense of betrayal by G-d and their parents, who assigned them a certain gender at birth. By inhabiting their full truth, Andy opened into forgiveness, with new trust in the "G-d who fashioned [Andy] in the mother's womb," with "praise for [Andy's own] wondrous creation," whose blueprint G-d "shaped in a hidden place" (Psalms 139:13-15). Andy's shifting relationship with G-d powered their evolution with wonder and gratitude. And with that redemptive turn, Andy found themselves supporting others: Andy endured burning, and now their light shined bright.

Just as Andy's trans experience was a fulcrum for their personal spiritual journey, the trans community's collective wisdom offered depth and richness to nourish Andy's spiritual becoming. Andy was comforted to find that others of trans experience also felt alienated by religion and G-d, that others who forged chasms of trans identity learned adaptive emotional and spiritual patterns ready to be reconsidered in light of who they were becoming. Andy drew strength from discovering that their path was both uniquely their own and also part of an exquisite community tapestry. And thanks to Andy, I could sense a bit of what a Biblical Moses yearned to know in saying to G-d atop Sinai, "Show me Your way" (Exodus 33:13).

The Trans Angels at Eden's Doorstep

The first chapters of Genesis record the divinity of Creation and the divine forms, male and female, fashioned in G-d's image. When the first humans left Eden, G-d "caused the *kruvim* (cherubs) to dwell east of the Garden of Eden and the flaming sword *ha-mithapekhet* (turning itself), to guard the path of the Tree of Life" (Genesis 3:24). Over 2,000 years ago, our spiritual ancestors imagined that the "turning" described not the angelic sword but the angels themselves, "sometimes appearing as men, sometimes as women, sometimes spirits, sometimes angels" (Genesis Rabbah 21:9). For anyone who transitioned from assigned gender to gender of identity, this mystical perspective offers that their capacity to transition is sourced in the sacred.

This angelic midrash also offers that society's path to full communion with the sacred, which Jewish mystical tradition calls the Garden of Eden, the garden of eternal and complete spiritual connection, leads society precisely toward trans life. Far from off the path, trans life is an essential part of that journey for everyone. It might even be, contrary to centuries of traditional exegesis, that Eden's "trans angels" do not block humanity's way back to Eden, but rather help show the way.

Our trans siblings have much to teach, and we cisgendered allies have much to learn. Show us your ways.

Chesed, Loving Connection: the Foundation of Allyship

Rabbi Marc Margolius

In Jewish mystical tradition, the first week of the Omer (the period between Passover and Shavuot), corresponds to the *sephirah* (Divine quality) of *Chesed*, Loving Connection, the Divine quality permeating and sustaining all of Creation as a seamless, unbroken whole. Because Jewish tradition understands all human beings are "stamped" with the Divine Image, it considers each of us imbued with *Chesed,* the G-dly trait enabling us to intuit and perceive the underlying, fundamental interrelatedness of all beings.

Chesed constantly flows within, around, and through us all, instilling in our consciousness what might be called "ocean awareness:" our capacity to sense that we and all beings are inextricably connected in an unbroken, single, web of aliveness. "We are caught in an inescapable network of mutuality, tied in a single garment of destiny," taught Dr. Martin Luther King Jr. in his *Letter from a Birmingham Jail.* "Whatever affects one directly, affects all indirectly."

Chesed enables those who enjoy privilege to function as an ally to marginalized communities by standing for and with them. It enables us to identify with the struggles of others, and simultaneously support them not by utilizing privilege to act on behalf of the marginalized, but rather by attuning ourselves to their perspectives and needs: by listening to rather than speaking for, by inquiring rather than presuming.

The Torah recognizes how the common roots and interconnectedness of the ever-diversifying human family immerses us and obligates us in a web of mutual responsibility. It calls upon us to "love our neighbor as ourselves," to understand our neighbor as us, and vice-versa. But it counsels us as well to act upon our responsibilities towards each other not by imposing ourselves upon others, but by honoring the inherent worth and unique perspective of those we support.

For example, in Deuteronomy 15:7-8, the Torah not only teaches us to respond to the needs of others, but to prioritize the expressed views and needs of the more vulnerable partner:

כִּי־יִהְיֶה בְךָ אֶבְיוֹן מֵאַחַד אַחֶיךָ בְּאַחַד שְׁעָרֶיךָ בְּאַרְצְךָ
אֲשֶׁר־ה' אֱלֹהֶיךָ נֹתֵן לָךְ לֹא תְאַמֵּץ אֶת־לְבָבְךָ וְלֹא תִקְפֹּץ
אֶת־יָדְךָ מֵאָחִיךָ הָאֶבְיוֹן: כִּי־פָתֹחַ תִּפְתַּח אֶת־יָדְךָ לוֹ
וְהַעֲבֵט תַּעֲבִיטֶנּוּ דֵּי מַחְסֹרוֹ אֲשֶׁר יֶחְסַר לוֹ:

If, however, there is a needy person among you, one of your kin in any of your settlements in the land that the Holy One your G-d is giving you, do not harden your heart and shut your hand against your needy kin. Rather, you must open your hand and lend that person sufficient for *whatever they need.*

The medieval Biblical commentator Rashi interprets the phrase "whatever they need" to mean that in supporting another human being, an "ally" should be guided not by what they believe is best for the recipient of the support, but rather by the subjective desires and needs of the one to whom one is allied.[3]

Rabbi Shlomo Wolbe, a great 20th century master of the Mussar (Jewish ethical) tradition, elaborates on this approach in his masterwork, *Alei Shur.* He teaches that when we choose to support our fellows, to ally ourselves with them, our initial inclination may be to focus on our *similarities* to those with whom we are allied. Our natural tendency, he says, is to see others as a mirror image of ourselves, whose needs must be the same as our own. Therefore, in our predilection to look for commonalities rather than distinctions, we may imagine we know what others need, perhaps even better than they know their own needs.

But according to Rabbi Wolbe, "[j]ust as people's temperaments are different, so are their needs." One who seeks to support others through the sacred quality of *Chesed* "needs to first of all learn to see and listen for what the other is lacking ... to understand how others are different from us and to search for what they lack, and not

---

3 Rashi's actual comment on "*asher yechsar lo*, that which they lack:" "Even a horse to ride on and a slave to run in front."

what we lack."[4] It is for this reason that the Torah stresses that the benchmark for supporting others is determined not by the view of the supporter, but by the *subjective, expressed need of the one receiving support.*

In sum, allyship grounded in the middah of *Chesed*, Loving Connection, involves (1) remembering the unbreakable interconnectedness of all life, (2) identifying and deepening our sense of kinship and connection with others, (3) cultivating deep curiosity about and sensitivity to others' historical experience and needs, and (4) commitment to hearing, learning from, and being guided by those to whom we are allied. It requires humility, the ability and willingness not to know, to be aware of and to relinquish privilege, while simultaneously remaining committed to and aligned with those we support.

In pursuing justice in solidarity with marginalized communities, may we be motivated and guided by *Chesed*, by Loving Connection: may we grow in awareness of the sacred diversity constantly emerging from the singular, vibrant, sacred "inescapable network of mutuality" in which we dwell.

---

4 Translation of *Alei Shur* by Rabbi David Jaffe in his "Tikkun Middot Project Curriculum for Adults," published by the Institute for Jewish Spirituality (2014)

When the Teacher Sweeps Your Floor

Rabbi Rena Singer

Allyship is an extraordinary weapon in the fight against loneliness. When we show up for each other's needs and vulnerabilities in ways that recognize the humanity of our friends and allies, we declare our commitment to camaraderie. We recognize that togetherness is one of the most effective solutions to our feelings of fragility and disempowerment. We become an embodied network, stretching beyond ourselves, supporting one another other with fierceness and resolve. This showing up is called allyship, but as a builder of connection and a fight against loneliness, it is also a way of partnering with G-d.

The story of Rabbi Akiva visiting his sick student is a story of *chesed* (graceful kindness) and also provides a fantastic model for allyship. In the Talmud, section Nedarim 39b-40a teaches a story about Rabbi Akiva, who was one of the most famous and powerful rabbis of his time. He learns that one of his students has fallen ill and that nobody has gone to visit him. Rabbi Akiva realizes that he must go visit the sick student himself and once he arrives, he sees that the student's floors are dirty. Rabbi Akiva arranges for the student's floors to be swept and cleaned. The text tells us that because of the way that Rabbi Akiva showed up for this student, because he made sure that the student's house was clean, the student experienced a miraculous recovery.

This story models allyship so well because it binds together power and humility. Rabbi Akiva, as a famous rabbi of his time, sees a problem in the just world he seeks to build. His job is to teach Jewish morals and ethics and laws, and yet when the time comes to enact those values, his students fail. He realizes that the most effective way to teach them is by showing up himself. He subverts the expectations for someone in his position, someone who is often perceived as too important, too powerful, too busy, and he does the work. He not only checks in on the sick student, his presence normalizes that act of allyship for others.

Once at his student's house, Rabbi Akiva does not do what he does best. He does not stay within his comfort zone, delivering a lecture or laying out a lesson plan. He surveys the situation for what is actually needed. He puts aside his ego, and asks, "What do you need? How can I help?" He understands that the student doesn't need a hero or a savior or even a brilliant rabbi, he just needs someone to help him clean up.

Our job as people who aspire to be great allies is to have the humility to ask "how can I help?" and really mean it. Helpfulness is tricky. We are taught that helpfulness should come naturally to "good people," yet we often get it wrong. Suddenly, we're the burden. If we can work on letting go of our need to feel powerful and knowledgeable and right, we can be great allies. If we can be brave enough to stick our necks out, yet smart enough to listen, we can show people that they are not alone.

As allies we become partners with G-d because the work of using our power and our humility to support one another leads to a world with more holy connection. But the work doesn't have to be difficult. Sometimes, all it takes is the bravery to show up and the wisdom to bring a good broom.

Unto Whose Hands Will This Victory Be Delivered?: Allyship in 2021 Through the Lens of Deborah the Prophetess

Rabbi Megan GoldMarche

The first paper I remember writing in Hebrew school was about Deborah the prophetess. I loved that there was a woman prophet. I loved her story and the image of her sitting under her own palm tree, giving out wisdom. This story, found in the book of Judges, is also famous for its ally, the general Barak, who when sent off to battle by Deborah says, "If you will go with me, I will go; if not, I will not go" (Judges 4:8).

As a feminist child, this made me love Barak. He knew Deborah was the leader of the people and he wanted to share the military victory with her. But later I wondered, is this what Deborah wanted to hear from Barak? And rereading it again, I am still unsure. Her reply, "Very well, I will go with you. However, there will be no glory for you in the course you are taking, for then the LORD will deliver Sisera into the hands of a woman" (Judges 4:9), seems to imply that he will be punished for needing her presence. Or perhaps there is a different, more implicit message: if you want someone marginalized by your side for the fight be ready to put them at the center. Or as I have often been told in my quest to do more racial justice work, "Nothing about us without us," but learn to do much of the work without always relying on us.

This is a very complicated message at first glance, and at least in my mind, on second and third glances as well. Do we always need to rely on marginalized folks to begin working towards justice? No! We can educate ourselves with pre-existing resources and we can learn from people of our own backgrounds who have already done the work and can serve as guides. But even in these moments we must put the voices and experiences of those who have been silenced at the center. As a white queer Jewish woman this all rings true in my head but when it comes to doing it, I often feel at a loss. While fighting for women's rights or LGBTQ rights feels natural, because my identity is at the center, fighting for racial justice feels just as necessary, if not more so, but the path feels less clear.

I am pretty sure I was never really taught how to be an ally. I was taught to lead. I was taught to see and name injustice, but not to step back and ask those who were most impacted by that lack of justice what they needed from me. I was taught to raise my voice, use my power, shine my light. But it was not until the end of rabbinical school that I remember thinking, "I have no idea how to be an ally in the fight for racial justice." My friends and I would go to rallies and be told, "Don't be too loud, let others lead the chants. Stand back or put yourselves between the police and people of color." I was a rabbi in training and I wanted to preach, to lead, not to wait to be called on. But a part of me understood that this too was leadership, just one for which I was ill-prepared.

I wish that I could tell you that since then I have figured it all out. Instead all I can say is I am still learning. And so today I wish I knew of Deborah's story so I could more fully understand what allowed for this woman to become "Deborah, wife of Lappidoth, a prophetess who led Israel at that time" (Judges 4:4). While seven women (and forty-eight men) are given prophet status by the rabbis, only Deborah and Hulda are called prophets in their time. Yet in the text we learn so little about Deborah. Even more astounding is that when reading the chapters of her story, the male ally Barak gets mentioned more than she does. Often we get so focused on allyship we almost erase the people we came to support. But real allyship should hold up the most marginalized voices, never displace them. True allyship is rarely filled with glory. As Deborah told Barak: if you want me by your side you are going to have to get out of the way when it comes to the victory. And so this is what I ask myself when I am trying to be an ally: do I need the glory? If the answer is yes, then I better get out of the way now. But if I can keep working, bit by bit, waiting to be asked or educating my own community with what I know, planning and attending racial justice events, marching in the background, maybe, just maybe, I will warrant the Lord delivering an end to racism to the hands of people of color. If that can be my goal, to be a soldier in that war, not the victor, not the hero, then maybe I will merit to play a small part in that victory. But if Deborah shows up and says stop waiting for me, I need you to go on your own, I also need to be ready to rise up and march, to take the risk, and not worry whose name ends up in the history books.

For You Were Also Strangers: The Sacred Purpose of Empathy

Rabbi Steven Philp

In our work to heal the brokenness of this world, fault lines have emerged within and between marginalized communities. The hard-earned coalitions that brought people of diverse backgrounds together at Seneca Falls, Selma, and Stonewall have started to rupture. Common cause no longer serves as the tie that binds us. The competing parades and marches of the past few years show that focus has turned to our differences and disagreements. This is not to delegitimize the critiques we may levy against each other; we can and must address behavior that perpetuates harm. Yet rather than inviting each other into conversation, we sever association.

There seems to be a prevailing belief that allyship, particularly with those whose stance on important issues may be different from your own, comes at the cost of one's ethical integrity. And there is a troubling understanding that to commit one's energy to the betterment of others means the persistence of your own marginalization. The result is that communities who ought to be walking hand-in-hand toward the promise of a more equitable world attempt the same journey alone.

This fragmentation is the product of a scarcity mindset. We have been taught that the resources for substantive change are in short supply. Certainly, the message from those in power is that the mechanisms of justice are limited and to satisfy one demand is to deny the advancement of another. Yet the perception that there is only so much to go around has been used to divide and disenfranchise marginalized communities throughout history. It is embedded in our political rhetoric, pitting farmers and factory workers against immigrants, women against their trans siblings, or Jews against communities of color – and while we fight over access to the American Dream, those already enjoying the privileges of this country remain untouched.

A scarcity mindset teaches that if we take time to help others, the issues that directly impact our lives will be forgotten. So we become afraid. Fear drives us to close ranks and turn inward, devoting our time and energy to tend to our own wounds. We zealously guard the borders of our community, quick to decide who is in and who is out by submitting each other to tests of ideological purity. We ask in the spirit of Rabbi Hillel: if we are not for ourselves, who will be? We worry that the answer may be "no one," and forget his warning that we will lose our humanity if we are only for ourselves (Pirkei Avot 1:14). Consumed by our own history of pain, we deaden our empathic impulse, no longer able to recognize and relate to the suffering of others. Where we once found a companion to share this burden, we can only see a threat.

Yet empathy is inherent to who we are. Our biology enables us to experience the emotions of others simply by observing them. It is the genetic inheritance that makes laughter contagious, helps us celebrate and mourn together, and allows us to share our pain. Fear may dull this empathic impulse, but we are also able to cultivate and hone it. This is the inheritance of our tradition, one that recalls a history of discrimination and violence to orient us toward a more just, more hopeful future. The Torah reminds us, "You know the soul of the stranger for you were also strangers" (Exodus 23:9). Through ritual and liturgy, we reenact the moments that our people have stood on the margins of society, whether as slaves in Egypt or refugees on the shores of this country. We do not remember these stories to reinforce distrust of those outside our community. Instead, the residual pain of the past calls us toward every place where brokenness persists today. Judaism teaches us that our wounds are a source of courage and vision; they give purpose and direction to our empathic impulse, directing us toward allyship with other marginalized communities.

To affirm the humanity of those who are unlike us is a radical and countercultural act. Yet the claim that all people are beings of inherent worth and inalienable dignity is fundamental to Judaism, encoded in the first few verses of our sacred texts:

"And G-d created humankind in the divine image, in the image of G-d was humankind made" (Genesis 1:27). In a world that teaches us to distrust people outside our immediate circle, it takes a conscious and deliberate effort to bridge the fear that pulls us apart and uncover that fragment of divinity embedded within each other.

When describing the *mishkan*, the portable synagogue and community center that our ancestors carried with them on their forty-year journey through the wilderness, the Torah teaches us that the presence of G-d manifested at a particular point within it: between two angelic figures of hammered gold, who stood facing each other with wings spread open (Exodus 25:22). For the rabbis, these angels symbolized the sacred power of relationship: an intimate and vulnerable space that opens us to encounter with the divine (TB Sanhedrin 7a). If we are to recognize and honor the part of each other that is a reflection of G-d, we must adopt a similar posture: unlearning habits shaped by fear and shedding the assumptions we have made about each other, allowing ourselves instead to see the tender and wounded places within our neighbor and letting them see us in kind.

Allyship refuses the distortions of a scarcity mindset, understanding that the promise of a more equitable world draws closer when we walk this journey together. Judaism teaches us that our wounds are the foundation for a radical and countercultural empathy, allowing us to recognize and address the pain of the other, particularly, and most powerfully, those with whom we disagree. In choosing conversation over disassociation, we come to understand that ours is a shared future, one in which the divine fragment inherent to all people is cherished and respected. And we find that in coming together, allies in the fight for justice, there has been abundance all along: of strength, of courage, and of hope.

Shifrah and Puah Were Egyptian

Rabbi Mira Beth Wasserman, Ph.D.

The Exodus is among the greatest stories of struggle and liberation, and at first glance, the place of allies is hard to find. In the standard telling, translated into hundreds of languages, the enslaved Israelites languish for generations, their burdens increasing as Pharaoh's brutalities grow harsher, until G-d at long last hears their cries and sends Moses to lead them. But before the wonders and the plagues, before the sea opens up and G-d's justice brings Pharaoh low, ordinary people take extraordinary risks to resist Pharaoh and protect the Israelites. In the very first chapter of the Book of Exodus, before Moses is born, two midwives named Shifrah and Puah refuse Pharaoh's orders to kill the Israelites' newborn sons. Jewish tradition and translators and commentators of other faiths all presume Shifrah and Puah were Israelites. In fact the original Hebrew is not at all clear. There is good reason to think that Shifrah and Puah are Egyptian. In this reading, Shifrah and Puah and their acts of resistance inscribe the redemptive power of allyship into the Bible's foundational story of liberation.

As the Book of Exodus begins, the children of Jacob who settled in Egypt generations before have grown into a populous group. Even in the midst of their enslavement and oppression, their numbers continue to grow, and Pharaoh and his people feel threatened. According to Exodus 1:16, Pharaoh charges the two midwives Shifrah and Puah to enact a genocidal plan, instructing them, "When you deliver the Hebrew women, look at the birthstool: if it is a boy, kill him; if it is a girl, let her live."

Who were these two midwives? The Hebrew text identifies them as "*meyaldot ha-'ivriyot*." In all the standard translations, this is rendered "the Hebrew midwives," with "*'ivriyot*," or "Hebrew" understood as an adjective modifying "*meyaldot/*midwives." But Hebrew grammar allows for another equally plausible translation, in which the term "*meyaldot ha-'ivriyot*" is a construct of two nouns and means "the midwives *of* the Hebrews." In this rendering, Shifrah and Puah are not identified as Israelites themselves, but are rather workers of unspecified backgrounds whose job it is to attend Israelite women giving birth. On the basis of the Hebrew alone, there is no reason to choose one translation over the other. The standard translation has shaped our understanding of this story for hundreds of years. It is time to consider the other possibility.

To be clear, Shifrah and Puah are heroes, whatever their background. Fearing G-d, they refuse Pharaoh's decree, protecting the lives of the infants that he would have them murder. He takes note of their insubordination and summons them to answer for their actions. Called back to

Pharaoh's court, Shifrah and Puah dissemble, claiming that Hebrew women are not like Egyptian women; strong as animals, they give birth themselves before the midwives even arrive (Exodus 2:19). It is a measure of Pharaoh's chauvinism that he accepts this explanation unquestioningly; he has already reduced the Israelites to subhuman status and so can readily believe that they are a species apart. The midwives effectively deploy Pharaoh's bigotry in their own defense. They risked everything to save the Israelite babies and through their own cleverness, they narrowly escape with their lives. Whether we understand them as Israelite or Egyptian, Shifrah and Puah offer a rare example of courage and principle in the way they put the lives of others above their own.

If we follow all the commentaries and translations in understanding Shifrah and Puah as Israelites themselves, their courage is not only an act of piety and principle, it expresses their sense of solidarity with their own people. In refusing to submit to Pharaoh's decree, they act to protect their community and its future. They risk their own individual lives for the sake of future generations.

The other possibility, that Shifrah and Puah are not Israelites, has scarcely been entertained in the long history of Biblical interpretation, and it holds out a more audacious possibility. In this version of events, the midwives are in no way personally threatened by Pharaoh's designs. They have nothing to gain from frustrating Pharoah's decree, and everything to lose. Pharaoh's decree does not endanger their loved ones, but their active resistance to it does. If Shifrah and Puah are Egyptians, their motivations cannot be explained in terms of self-interest on any level. They are moved instead by what is right and holy. If we allow ourselves to imagine Shifrah and Puah as Egyptians, we can recognize that theirs is a story that celebrates solidarities across lines of ethnicity, status, and identity. Though Shifrah and Puah are people whom the Pharaonic system privileges and protects, they nevertheless choose to stand with those who are oppressed and imperiled.

Why is it that this version of the story is not the one that has been passed down? Why do the commentaries and translators stop short of even imagining a possibility that the Hebrew text holds out? What accounts for the failure of Jewish traditions of interpretation to depict Shifrah and Puah as righteous Egyptians, as radicals resisting Egyptian oppression from within, as allies?

I would guess that the failures of history forestalled and constrained the Jewish interpretive imagination. Had our early history held out examples of non-Jews putting themselves out for Jews, taking real risks, perhaps our commentators might have considered the possibility. To be sure, the ancient and medieval past includes examples of non-Jews extending protection and toleration to Jews, of defending Jewish claims to life and livelihood, but for the most part, the Jews' best defenders have been kings and nobles, people in power with nothing to lose. In the long history of our people, there are few precedents for the righteous gentiles who risked their lives and the lives of their families to save Jews from Nazi destruction during the Shoah. If history had been different, perhaps it would have been easier for our forebears to imagine Egyptian midwives risking death to save Israelite babies.

Today, new historical realities enlarge our imagination. We can imagine the righteous Shifrah and Puah as Egyptians, because we have learned that care and trust and friendship and love cross all lines of separation. We have seen allies take risks for us, some because of principles of justice and truth, others because of bonds of caring and connection. The story of the Egyptian midwives is a story for anyone who could recede into self-protection, but instead chooses to step outside of their own comfort and safety, and to take risks for another.

Two caveats: First, when I claim Shifrah and Puah as exemplary allies, I am not suggesting that to be an ally, one must risk all. Just as one can aspire to leadership without claiming to be another Moses, so too one can aspire to allyship without sacrificing all. Second, in my interpretation, it is Shifrah and Puah's Egyptian identities that are important, not their roles as midwives. I am not suggesting that the role of midwife provides a helpful metaphor for thinking about allyship. On the contrary: allies share in the labor of liberation and have no special status or expertise that allows them to "deliver" others.

Ultimately, the risks that Shifrah and Puah embraced are not greater than those of the Israelites they served. I like to think they could not imagine doing otherwise, that there was no calculus of risk and benefit, no scales on which the risk to themselves was weighed against the heft of their principles. The choice of life, of justice, of compassion was so clear that it could scarcely be considered a choice. And this might be what it means to be an ally in their image: to live such that a threat to any other is an offense to oneself, so that it is the very notion of self-interest that becomes foreign.

Divine Community: Allyship and the Unity of One G-d

Rabbi Rahel Berkovits

I strive to be an ally, not despite being a religious Jew, but rather because I am a religious Jew. My understanding of what it means to live with in a Jewish community and to always be striving towards a relationship with the Divine in this world requires me to see the image of the Divine within each and every human being that I encounter. One can only see the sparks of the Divine image within another being if one gets to know them by listening to their story and trying to understand how they experience the world. As each individual is unique and different, a testament to that Divine spark within them, then surely people will experience the world differently from each other. The key is to truly "see" the other for who they are and to acknowledge that experience as an encounter with the Divine. In my view, to ignore the plight of another person just because their experience in this world is different from your own is a rejection of the essence of the community of Israel, who is a testament to the fact that G-d is One.

I see this idea presented in the teachings of *Hazal,* in the laws concerning the recitation of the *Shema*. The second chapter of Mishnah *Berakhot* interrupts the flow of cases which deal with the

manner in which one recites the *Shema* to discuss
human interruptions during the powerful
experience of proclaiming G-d's unity in the
world. Mishnah *Berakhot* 2:1 discusses the
situation in which one person is reciting the
Shema and they encounter another human being.
May one pause in the middle of the *Shema*
recitation and initiate a greeting? May one
respond to a greeting of another while reciting the
Shema? The text explains:

בַּפְּרָקִים שׁוֹאֵל מִפְּנֵי הַכָּבוֹד וּמֵשִׁיב, וּבָאֶמְצַע
שׁוֹאֵל מִפְּנֵי הַיִּרְאָה וּמֵשִׁיב, דִּבְרֵי רַבִּי מֵאִיר.
רַבִּי יְהוּדָה אוֹמֵר, בָּאֶמְצַע שׁוֹאֵל מִפְּנֵי הַיִּרְאָה,
וּמֵשִׁיב מִפְּנֵי הַכָּבוֹד, בַּפְּרָקִים שׁוֹאֵל מִפְּנֵי
הַכָּבוֹד, וּמֵשִׁיב שָׁלוֹם לְכָל אָדָם :

At the breaks [between sections of the
Shema], one may greet [another person]
because of honor and return a greeting. In
the middle [of a section], one may greet
[another] because of fear and return a
greeting. These are the words of R. Meir. R.
Yehuda says: In the middle [of a section],
one may greet [another] because of fear
and return a greeting because of honor. At
the breaks [between sections of the
Shema], one may greet because of honor
and return a greeting [lit. *Shalom*] to any
person [*kol adam*].

R. Meir and R. Yehuda disagree as to the
specifics of for whom one may interrupt and at

50

which point during the recitation of the *Shema* one may do so; however, they both acknowledge that one does pause to balance one's relationship with the Divine and one's relationship with the surrounding community. The first and central line of the *Shema* itself incorporates this tension as the individual addresses not G-d, as with prayer, but the community of Israel: "*Shema Yisreal*".

To greet and to inquire about the well-being [*Shalom*] of another human being means to recognize the other as being worthy of your concern and acknowledgment. To disregard their greeting as they stand before you would cause them great pain and hurt. The Mishnah seems to be saying that it would be impossible to fully proclaim G-d's oneness in the world and reside in a holy domain (*Malhut Shamayim*, the Kingdom of Heaven, as the Mishnah describes the experience of *Shema* in the continuation of the chapter) if one were to directly ignore standing in front of one's eyes another human being, who is created in the image of G-d. One cannot fully know G-d and proclaim G-d's unity in this world without knowledge of the well-being of the other members of the community. One does not truly understand the oneness of the Divine if one can disconnect from the pain of other human beings and have no concern for their welfare.

R. Yehuda's language of returning a greeting of peace and wellbeing to any person clearly mirrors the language used in the last mishnah of the entire tractate of *Berakhot* which states:

וְהִתְקִינוּ, שֶׁיְּהֵא אָדָם שׁוֹאֵל אֶת שְׁלוֹם חֲבֵרוֹ
בַּשֵּׁם, שֶׁנֶּאֱמַר (רות ב) וְהִנֵּה בֹעַז בָּא מִבֵּית לֶחֶם,
וַיֹּאמֶר לַקּוֹצְרִים יְיָ עִמָּכֶם, וַיֹּאמְרוּ לוֹ, יְבָרֶכְךָ
יְיָ.

And they [the Rabbis] decreed that a person should greet [*shoel shalom*] one's friend with the Name [of G-d], as it says, Then Boaz came from Bethlehem, and said to the reapers '*HaShem* is with you', and they said to him 'May *HaShem* bless you'. [Ruth 2:4]

Not only should the recitation of *Shema* acknowledge others in the wider community, but, when one greets another person one should turn that greeting into a statement about the Divine in the world. Asking another individual about themselves, finding out if they are at peace or feel whole (*S-L-M*) and how they are doing is an encounter worthy of invoking G-d's name in this world because one is seeing a facet of the Divine image in their responses. The two statements of "G-d is one" and "Hello, how are you?" are really mirror images of the other, part and parcel of one single Jewish belief statement about creating a holy community defined and unified by faith in one G-d. Although nowadays we do not customarily use G-d's name in greeting others nor do we interrupt the recitation of the *shema*, the message of communal concern and acknowledging the Divine in all human beings presented by Mishnah *Berakhot* still strongly resonates and should inform our behavior towards others. Allyship is a religious imperative as we are all linked through the oneness of the Divine.

Hand Raised High/ Passover Midrash 2021

Rabbi Amichai Lau-Lavie

וּבְנֵי יִשְׂרָאֵל יֹצְאִים בְּיָד רָמָה

"The people of Israel left with their hand raised high" (Exodus 14:8).

"When I found I had crossed that line, I looked at my hands to see if I was the same person. There was such a glory over everything; the sun came like gold through trees, and over the fields, and I felt like I was in Heaven" (Harriet Tubman).

"The exodus began, but is far from having been completed" (Rabbi Abraham Joshua Heschel).

What if she had not stretched her hand?
What if she had not stretched her hand to risk and reach and save that baby in the basket?
What if she chose, like so many of us often do, to play it safe?

Seder Scene #1: Slow Motion
The Princess of Egypt, mid-bathing on the river Nile, notices, raises and extends her arm, instantly becoming a legend. Using her privilege to defy

oppression, she shows up to do her part in the ongoing work of liberation.

When you get to Maggid at your Seder, here's a fresh add-on: tell her tale and then embody. Try out her extended gesture as you imagine it. It's also a good mid-Seder stretch.

How long can you/we keep the arm extended?

What will we learn from her this year on how to keep becoming allies? Can we keep extending our arms to one another? Do we commit to live, and leave the narrow place, together, with "our hand raised high"?

Seder Scene #2: Eye Contact

A moment later, four eyes meet in recognition of shared purpose. The princess and the enslaved girl, brave big sister: two allies conspiring to help one life, to save the people.

The Latin origin of 'conspiracy' suggests the act of breathing together. To conspire is to be this close to trust. Breath to breath. Eye to Eye. The ever-evolving 'we' is the recurring commitment.

Try it at Seder. Role play this brief scene with two people, no words, just eye contact, imagining this moment of multiple meanings, then and now. (It will be weird on Zoom but fascinating). Take turns. Discuss. What if Passover 2021 is not just one more reading of the same old saga but the taking on of real commitment, individual, communal, to lean-in and to reach out as better allies?

This year, with many in the Jewish community more aware and activated to join the fight against systemic injustice, how do we go beyond the bondage of our past, to rise up with this sacred story as another roadmap for the continued exodus of our society's moral evolution?

What if the will to fight for freedom doesn't end with Passover? Perhaps that's why our ancients came up with the Counting of the Omer, 49 nights of persistence. We walk each year in our ancestors' footsteps. From the day they left the narrowness, with hands raised high until they reached the mountaintop of unity and purpose. Our journey picks up where they left off, each year again, from one threshold to another, Passover to Shavuot is the continued counting of the daily commitment to walk the talk of liberation, failing, restarting, again and again. Seven weeks of practice, each day another way to keep extending ourselves, more accountable, choosing to show up, to listen, to support.

When we complete the count it's Shavuot and we stay up late again, just like on Seder night, to delve in deeper to the stories that guide our lives. The tale of Ruth the Moabite is told, a scroll of loving kindness, where hands and eyes touch, strangers are welcomed, hunger held by care. Ruth, Naomi, and Boaz reminded us not to give up on each other.

What if we pay closer attention to these sacred stories, and recommit to this ritual rhythm of our life? To keep on walking, marching, counting, and conspiring for change, from one holy night to another, year and after year, hand in hand, raised high, until nobody is left behind.

What if we choose to stretch our hand?

On the Path to Sinai, My Ally Becomes My Sister

Rabbi Susan Talve

The great suffering caused by the plagues was the consequence, like Camus's plague, of years of enslaving others for free labor. We learned that it took the suffering of the people in power to finally free the slaves (Ex.12:33). Pharaoh would have to hold his dead son in his arms to end the plague of structural institutional racism. But before he let us go, he warned us, "*raah neged p'nechem*," "evil will go before your faces," (Ex. 10:10) warning us that there would always be the chance that we would go through all that suffering and become worse than Pharaoh and the chance for change would be lost. We learned that our challenge would be to create a whole new way of relating to each other where the command to love the stranger would take down the structures that make racial divisions necessary. We would need to make laws that promoted equity and rejected any possibility of constructing communities where some mattered more than others.

The journey from the Sea to Sinai, from Passover to Shavuot, gave us time to be ready to receive the Torah, a guide to equity and a new way of walking in the world. We would not do this alone. We would have to learn to love the stranger; not tolerate, not abide or just reside with, but love. And we learned that love, too, would require time to listen and to learn and a spiritual practice that would challenge us again and again to not let fear or greed or self-interest harden our hearts.

Not long after an unarmed Black teenager named Mike Brown was murdered, another teen was killed by a police officer. Those of us who had been gathering each night in Ferguson to hold the whole biased system of law enforcement accountable got in our cars and drove to the scene of the most recent crime. We were an unlikely group of allies of young Black Lives Matter protesters, clergy of all faiths, parents who had lost their children to gun violence and citizens who saw the connections between the targeting and suffering of Black and Brown people on our streets to those across the globe, including the Palestinians. When we arrived, Reverend Traci Blackmon, an African-American UCC minister and leader of our protest movement, and I approached the parents of Vonderrit Myers. The police were preparing to take the body to the morgue. Reverend Blackmon and I accompanied Vonderrit's father and the body. We wanted to make sure that both were treated with dignity and respect and that there would be no covering up how this young man was killed. When we returned to the neighborhood, Rev. Traci led us in prayer over the blood-stained grass, declaring it hallowed ground. I offered the midrash that taught while Moses was praying for the sea to part, Nachshon dared to jump in. I explained that we usually attribute the parting of the sea to the chutzpah of that young man but I added that I believed it was the whole community of adults that jumped in after that child. Not just his family, but all of us, willing to risk our lives for each other's children. As I was preparing to leave Vonderrit's mother, Sarita, looked into my soul, and made me promise, "Don't let them make a thug out of my son, Rabbi." I promised her that awful night that I would be her ally and that I would continue to make sure that her son was treated with dignity. I continue telling the story to keep my promise to her. I continue working to break down the structures of oppression created by the institutionalized white supremacy that built this nation; structures that are getting stronger with the hate and violence of white nationalism. I continue teaching that there is a need and a reason for race in America (just as it was for Hitler) and that Black bodies still fuel the fires under the melting pot of the failing American project. I continue telling the truth that Black and Brown bodies just don't matter as much in the construct of white America and that the legacy of slavery has built a conspiracy of shame that dehumanizes people of color and sets us up to blame the victim with thug language that continues to be used to distract us from mourning the lives of Mike Brown, Tamir Rice, Breonna Taylor and Vonderrit Myers and so many others. Thug language is a shaming of the victim that is used to get the people in power off the hook for using systems of oppression for their own self-interest, and we will not have it.

My relationship with Rev. Blackmon deepened that night. We carried pain together. We held space for each other. We trusted our love and respect for each other enough to have difficult conversations on faith, on racism, anti-Semitism and on Israel and Palestine. At some point we were no longer allies; we were family. Our congregations fell in love and for years Christ the King used our home-baked challah for their communion bread. When my worst nightmare became real and we lost our youngest daughter to cancer, Rev. Traci was there and sang at her funeral. Adina's funeral was on the Monday of the Dr. King holiday. It was the first Dr. King community event I had missed since they started in the 80's. Most of that awful day is still a blur but though there were over a thousand people in attendance I remember seeing the diverse protest family, including the pro-Palestinian group that had targeted me for not being a vocal supporter of BDS. Showing up for each other and claiming all children as our own tore down old prejudices as we began to build a better way forward.

This period of the Omer prepares us each year for standing together at Sinai where we get a glimpse of *"ha kol,"* "the all," and we see that the distinctions between us are illusion. As we left the narrow place of slavery behind, we remembered Pharaoh's warning that we would never be free if we did to others what he did to us. We were committed to creating a whole new paradigm where there were no masters and slaves, no haves and have-nots and all lives truly mattered. We ate the matzah, the bread with no ego, to leave space for us to leave attachments behind and move forward with humility. We counted each day of the Omer, praying that the simple barley would keep us humble, keep us from falling back on the familiar structures that oppressed us and look forward to a whole new way of relating when truth is told with loving kindness, and justice and peace kiss (Ps. 85:11). And then, on the fiftieth day, when we reach the mountaintop, we become One, and we are able to eat that holy challah without getting puffed up ourselves and leave room to love the stranger until there is no other and from being trusted allies we remember that we are family.

Tzimtzum:
Allyship as Humility

Rabbi Dan Ornstein

The Zoom room fills up quickly with a color diversity more pronounced than at any time in my synagogue's history. We're here to confront the bleeding wound caused by this knifepoint moment in American history. We're coming to understand that progress's paper band aid has been ripped off, revealing the deep puncture of America's slave legacy that has never healed.

We crowd in on the screen with Black activists, Jews of color, people who struggle to live with, and within, the intersecting cultural bequests of race, Jewish history and religion. Among the panelists, two stand out, now-long-time members of my congregation with whom I've traveled complicated journeys into Jewish life and family. They'll both speak tonight about their experiences with racism and caste as Jews of color. I'm rightly proud of them, and I'm rightly proud of the role I've played in their lives.

Pride is a trickster. You nurse it unreflectively enough and it grows tentacles of smugness that lash you to wherever you're standing. In its grasp, you think you're moving upward, when all you're really doing is chasing your tail. This smugness is mine that night, but I don't acknowledge it just then. I politely feign attentiveness to speaker after speaker, but I'm above it all. I'm a good seventies/eighties Jewish liberal from a highly integrated Queens neighborhood, whose civil rights activist parents moved there to make sure my siblings and I learned to live respectfully with others in the world. Over a quarter of a century, I've had a hand in shaping a shul that doesn't talk diversity because we live it... (maybe). My wife and I are part of a racism study group, working hard at identifying and slowly leeching from our bones America's racist poison. I already know all of this racism stuff. Why really listen?

One of my former congregants begins to speak. She tells a story about walking out of our sanctuary during Shabbat services five years ago. She was accosted by another member, a self-appointed gatekeeper who politely feigned friendliness to check out who she was and what she was doing there. With no overt anger, but with the sadness of hurtful memory, she reflects upon that moment:

"I remember thinking to myself, 'Is this a racist synagogue? Why do I want to be here?'"

Now I'm listening...And I'm embarrassed...And I'm fuming.

Never mind that she's only being honest about her early experiences in White-Jewish America.

Never mind that she never says to the group, "Rabbi Ornstein and his synagogue are so racist!"

Never mind that she and her family are very happy members at that moment, five years later.

I'm listening and embarrassed and fuming: "What? After all I have personally done...after all we have personally done for you...We're *the*

64

embodiment of the old legend that all, A-L-L Jews, past, present, future, stood at Mount Sinai when the Torah was given...How could you...."

She finishes her monologue, then my second congregant speaks. He's another happy Jewish camper, another satisfied customer of Rabbi and Company, yet much more circumspect about his experiences. That circumspection drives me nuts. He declines to tell the group about what happened a year earlier when, as I led Friday night services in our chapel, one of our building staff gatekept him with a pleasant smile at the lobby doors. I only found out about this after worship was done, when both men, now chatting in genuinely friendly tones, joked about their "misunderstanding" out in the lobby. A misunderstanding that, turning on the wrong word or a misinterpreted gesture, could have become fatal.

It's what my congregant doesn't say which once again makes me embarrassed, makes me fume, makes me despondent that I, that we, didn't catch these encounters, didn't save these two of our fellow Jews from such "friendly welcoming."

I think, "With friendliness like this, who needs...."

"Who needs to rethink this monologue in your head?" I suddenly think to myself.

My two congregants' stories, the shared and the unshared, aren't about me, my reputation, and the outsize spaces we occupy.

They aren't about my leadership or my anything.

They aren't about our shul, good, bad, or racist.

They aren't even necessarily about how racist or anti-racist our sacred communal spaces are generally.

They're about my two congregants' struggles to allow Jewish identity and belonging to get under their skins, as they struggle every day to live in their skins without suffering harassment or hatred.

Now I'm actually listening. I've made a tiny space in my head, in my heart, in my piece of White polite society. For a tiny moment, I struggle toward the simple awareness necessary to step away and step back, so they can occupy the space they need, they deserve, to which they have an unconditional right.

The great Jewish mystic, Isaac Luria, wondered about the "back story" of creation found in the Book of Genesis. How could G-d, Who is everywhere, allow for the creation of the physical world which, by definition, is not G-d? He taught that G-d created the world through *tzimtzum*: self-contraction.

Prior to Creation, there was only the infinite creative light of G-d filling all existence. When it arose in G-d's Will to create worlds and emanate the emanated ... G-d contracted (in Hebrew "*tzimtzum*") G-d's self in the point at the center...so that there remained a void, a hollow empty space, away from the central point ... After this tzimtzum ... G-d drew down from the infinite creative light a single straight line... and it chained down, descending into that void. ... In the space of that void, G-d...made all the worlds. (— Etz Chaim, Arizal, Heichal A"K, anaf 2. Translation by chabad.org with modifications by Dan Ornstein).

One explanation of this complicated teaching is this. Before space and time and creation, there was nothing but G-d, so nothing besides G-d could exist. To give the world "breathing room" to become and to grow, G-d self-contracted just enough to leave a space into which G-d, as it were, injected a thin ray of infinitely creative light. Out of that holy light, that creative energy, the universe was born.

I'm most certainly not G-d. At times, I occupy too much space, so that I forget what it means to truly be myself. But right then, that night, not as a rabbi, not as a leader, but as my friends' fellow traveler, I'm learning to imitate G-d by engaging in my own *tzimtzum*, so their narratives, their truths can grow. I'm learning that being their ally requires, first of all things, finding the self-contracting humility to get out of their way.

Et Chata'ai Ani Mazkir HaYom / Today, I Acknowledge My Sins (Gen. 41:9)

Rabbi Menachem Creditor

It was the summer of 2007 and I had just moved to Berkeley, CA to begin work as rabbi of a vibrant synagogue. The possibilities felt endless. Among my greatest hopes was to forge strong and loving friendships with faith leaders in my neighborhood, to walk together with our communities in pursuit of societal justice. My first call was to Pastor Michael McBride, a Pentecostal Evangelical faith leader for a largely Black church situated across the street from my shul. I couldn't wait.

We set up a time to meet and grab coffee. As soon as we sat down, I launched right in: "Michael, I'm so glad we're meeting. Tell me what we can do for you."

His response remains one of my deepest moments of personal learning and spiritual growth: "Menachem, the first thing you can do is never speak to me like that again."

I was shocked by his words, and by the pain and anger in his eyes as he said them. What had I done wrong? How had I hurt my new friend's feelings? What had begun, for me, as a hopeful moment of connection was instantly something else, something much harder. I didn't understand.

So I asked him to say more. Perhaps I didn't actually say anything. I can't truly remember, but I can imagine that my face showed my soul's confusion and my worry that I had violated something important. I remember feeling very ashamed of myself without quite knowing why.

When I began our conversation by asking what "we" could do for "them," I didn't consider the implied power dynamics of my language. Here I was, a white man, a rabbi of a local synagogue, excited to offer aid to a person I had never met and to their community, assuming that what "they" needed "we" could provide. That's not how a loving relationship works, and that's not how justice will be achieved. That was the blindness of my privilege speaking, and a mistreatment of my neighbor, relegating him (however unintentionally) to less-than status in my own eyes. He had experienced this during his life, and was unwilling to be seen in this way. I didn't even know how I was seeing the world around me until it was pointed out by my new friend.

I learned on that day, and on many subsequent days, that only by spending real time together and learning of each other can any partnership truly begin. Allyship is an arduous practice of unlearning, of reassessing, of doing the hard work of re-understanding self and the other. It is, in fact, the fulfillment of the Torah's golden rule to "love your neighbor as yourself." How heavenly it is to do the earthly work of seeing myself more clearly in order to be of more humble service to my neighbor.

A famous quote from the famous scholar, artist, and activist Lilla Watson spells out my mistake that day and points to the essential dignity of my neighbors that I hadn't begun to see: "If you have come here to help me you are wasting your time, but if you have come because your liberation is bound up with mine, then let us work together."

Over the course of our time together, and through the many years we shared as neighbors, and, eventually as friends, Pastor McBride helped me begin to understand what my words had meant to him, and how I could be a better friend and ally. I had meant well; he knew that. He forgave me. That was important in ways I could never have understood before we met.

That holy day revealed the incompleteness of my sense of the world thus far, a deeper understanding of what allyship truly demands, and the possibility of deeper blessings ahead.

Coming Closer to Pride

Rabbi Raysh Weiss, Ph.D.

Arguably more than any other holiday on the Jewish calendar, Passover unifies the Jewish people through a commonly shared narrative of struggle and salvation. But as the trajectory of the Passover Haggadah so artfully reminds us, that narrative is far from a monolith; rather, the story we share is a trajectory marked by a dynamic transition from shame to pride. Our people started as idol worshippers and were later enslaved, only to find liberation eventually through G-d's redemptive benevolence and covenant.

Beginning on the second night of Passover, we embark on a seven-week spiritual journey, a precarious time in the Jewish historical imagination, marked by discord and mourning. The Talmud teaches us in BT Yevamot 61b that during this seven-week period following Passover, 12,000 pairs of the great 2nd century sage Rabbi Akiva died in one single day because they did not properly respect each other. This Hebrew year, 5781, also during this period, our annual weekly Torah reading cycle carries us from the Torah portion of *Shemini*, which recounts the tragic and untimely demise of Aaron's two sons, Nadav and Avihu, through the rest of Leviticus, which concerns itself with the delicate balance between purity and impurity, inclusion, and exclusion.

A particularly striking, and at first deeply unsettling, example of the Levitical concern to distinguish between insiders and outsiders can be found in this year's double-portion of Tazria-Metzora, which describes at length a condition in Hebrew called *tzaraat*, often translated as leprosy, which ultimately affected not only a person's skin, but also potentially one's home, clothes, vessels, and other material belongings. While the condition manifested itself physically, the Torah understands it as having a spiritual origin: that the so-called leper in this case is suffering this condition as a result of some personal failing. Leviticus carefully outlines how individuals afflicted with *tzaraat* must isolate themself until they are healed and can ultimately rejoin the community.

At first blush, this scenario is incredibly alarming and might even seem offensive to any of us who believe in social inclusion and human dignity. What does it mean for a society to forcibly eject people, both physically and spiritually? How can we derive any social inspiration today from such a seemingly judgmental and exclusive ancient ritual prescription? To appreciate the deeper meaning of this purification process and how its aims are not only healing, but also radical inclusion and compassion, we can turn to the Talmud.

In BT Moed Katan 5a, the rabbis describe the individual stricken with *tzaraat* as publicly declaring their state, crying out "Impure! Impure!" The Talmud goes on to explain that this declaration of impurity serves an important social and spiritual function. Upon hearing the individual's expression of deep pain, the Talmud explains, the community will be moved to pray for mercy for them. Instead of complete banishment and invisibility, the public is actively invited into relationship with the so-called leper, compassionately appealing to G-d on their behalf.

The image of the individual with tzaraat publicly disclosing that which is causing them the most shame is an incredibly powerful model for us to consider today. We can imagine the natural impulse of the individual afflicted with *tzaarat* to feel great shame upon their diagnoses and attempt to conceal their status for fear of how others may react and judge; in effect, self-exiling. Imagine a society in which marginalized people and communities are actively encouraged to express their vulnerability outwardly and feel safe doing so, without fear of external judgement and exclusion.

Being able to open up publicly and honestly about what most personally tortures our souls and our bodies and then to find solidarity and support in our neighbors is, indeed, the opposite of shame and isolation. What would it look like for us to feel comfortable sharing the parts about ourselves we feel most vulnerable? What would it look like to be greeted by a loving communal chorus of concern, support, and solidarity. When you are on your knees, what can the community do to support you and your loved ones?

That we should authentically and wholeheartedly pray alongside each other for the complete healing and acceptance of our neighbor is a central feature of a just and loving society and a key ingredient to what we today refer to as allyship. One of the goals of allyship is the overturning of social shame and stigma through affirming our common ground with genuine acts and expressions of compassion.

To be absolutely clear, I am not suggesting that someone who is marginalized because of their ideological, ethnic, racial, sexual, and/or class identity ought to feel shame; rather I am noting the ways in which members of marginalized groups can, and often do, feel completely alienated on the basis of their identity, which they then seek to conceal from the public for fear of being shunned. Reading today of the individual who bravely shares their vulnerability publicly and the community who lovingly holds them up, we should feel challenged to expand this category and apply it to our times, to imagine how we can create a public that is not only accepting but actively and lovingly concerns itself with the spiritual and physical health of its most vulnerable members. Reaching this point requires serious, on-the-ground work and the ability to hold our neighbor in as high regard as we hold ourselves and see ourselves in our neighbors. The scene of which we read cannot exist as merely a one-off performance of virtue, but rather, it must emerge from an ongoing context of developing those relationships.

Seen in this light, it feels especially fitting that in the seven weeks following Passover, the holiday which carries us from a space of shame to a space of pride, we think about the plight of the most spiritually and physically vulnerable individual in our society and unite as a community alongside them to pray for their well-being. Turning to both our Biblical example of *tzaraat* and the tragedy of Rabbi Akiva's pupils, we can better understand how divisions beget shame and shame begets divisions. The antidote to the mechanisms of division and shame is the bold and loving embrace of vulnerability and owning that about which we are most ashamed and the bold and loving embrace of vulnerability.

During this time of the Omer, we step outside of who we are in order to become who we need to be. We exist in community, only strengthened by the relationships we forge with our neighbors, casting our fate with theirs. We can't hate who we know.

Resiliency is Our Superpower

Rabbi Michael L. Moskowitz

In the blessing of the rabbinate, there are times we actively pursue our mission, understanding definitively why we advocate and share. But there also are times that our mission pursues us, reminding us why we do what we need to do, and, maybe even more importantly, teaching us why our faith has embedded within it such values for guidance in each and every instance. On a very personal level, such has been the case in being an ally and appreciating how significant this reality is.

It actually wasn't something on my radar. I believed ironically, it was obvious. I knew my beliefs of complete acceptance and support of LGBTQ+ individuals. In 1995, I saw it as an honor to stand under the chuppah with two women sharing their love with the community, in what we dreamed of being a legal wedding but back then could only be a commitment ceremony. While letters had been sent to the editors in the Jewish press opposing this occurring on our bima, we were steadfast in our support, resolute in knowing this was holy. Didn't our actions on that Saturday evening say it all?

Nearly 20 years later came the request to stand in front of the Federal Courthouse in Detroit rallying as the judge heard the landmark adoption case in which two women challenged Michigan's ban on same-sex marriage. Surprised that other rabbis refused to attend and speak at the gathering, organizers still believed it important for a Jewish message to be added to the rally. Following three other clergy, all of whom were gay, this straight rabbi ascended the podium. But who was I to speak following the eloquence and personal experience of those who preceded me? All I could reflect upon was the reality of the holiness found in my marriage, the blessings of my children. Knowing all of us to be created *B'tselem Elohim* (in the image of G-d), why shouldn't every individual be afforded this love, this joy? It was an unfamiliar crowd, but one that offered remarkable support. Unbeknownst to me, a young woman, a congregant of mine, had joined the gathering. She found me at the end and thanked me with words and hugs, her sister having recently come out. If only I understood at that moment what she was communicating.

Then there was the Shabbat after the attack on Pittsburgh's Jewish community, when eleven Jews were murdered in shul. Standing with us in solidarity, the Archbishop of Detroit shared from our pulpit, as did the Imam of the Islamic Center of America. The support and love felt both from the bima and in the pews was palpable. That morning, as I spoke of baseless hatred and the need to love all, honoring our diversity of religion and race, words were added to include sexual identity and the necessity to never discriminate. The strength and hope gained from that morning lifted us up in the midst of our pain. But once again, words privately shared after our morning prayers still resonate powerfully for me. In my mind, speaking of acceptance and adding to my remarks those in the LGBTQ+ community was natural. Yet, when a gay man thanked me specifically for this inclusion, what I believed to be obvious, was unexpected to many praying with us that day.

One might think that a rabbi would learn more quickly. But ultimately it was this year's pandemic that made the necessity of becoming an ally so pronounced. With additional time to study and share, some of my teachings incorporated these words of inclusion and acceptance specifically. A few discussions and lessons with Rabbi Mike Moskowitz that were conveyed to my congregation opened my eyes even more. And with comments publicly stated, articulating what I had believed and embraced for my entire rabbinate, the greater the response became. Watching individuals from the LGBTQ+ community repost my comments, share my teachings, affirm my beliefs, I realized it is not that I had said something so unique but that there are not enough allies in our world. What we do might seem obvious in resonating our beliefs, however, if we do not articulate it clearly, we are not demonstrating how important being an ally truly is.

The prophets of our faith cry out advocating for this reality. In recognizing the schisms and exclusions developing among the people Israel,

Isaiah declared "My house shall be a house of prayer for all people." There is no distinction here. All people. All of us are welcomed into our community. All of us deserve and feel the support and even love of community. And through that, all of us feel the support and love of G-d.

Why is it that two women, one of whom I have known for over 15 years, are so effusive when something positive and in support of the LGBTQ+ community, of their love, is made public at temple? Why is it that they both respond so quickly and affirmatively when their rabbis have done something lifting up this community? Again, for me, the words and these actions are what Judaism teaches. But for them, for far too many years, that is not what they have heard. Unfortunately so much of Judaism, of religion, has excluded, judged or at best remained silent. And a positive statement every couple years, at a service here or a rally there, is not enough. We cannot undo the wrongs of our past but we can make things right today by letting others know that we are allies; that we understand the importance in allyship.

In watching these women, their courage lifts me up. We cannot necessarily know the challenges felt and experienced, what they pushed through to find hope. To some degree, like the people of Israel, resiliency is their superpower. They persevere. They lift each other up. They exude positivity. Interesting that in being an ally we gain wisdom and insight from those we include. As a community, we gain strength from how they live with resilience.

For a couple of years, these two beautiful individuals have been trying to get pregnant. It has been difficult, fraught with challenges and setbacks. Last month though they announced their impending joy with excitement, and I responded in looking forward to the simcha that was on its way. Immediately the text shot back, "get ready for being in our lives for a long time." Finally, through this thick head I realized how important and even how blessed it is to be an ally. I realized you cannot say this too many times, ever. You are loved. And in being an ally, we help bring G-d into our world. Say these words to those in your lives. They need to be heard and affirmed. It makes us stronger as a people. And yes, some superpowers actually can be shared.

You Are Not Alone

Kohenet Keshira haLev Fife

On the evening of October 27, 2018, I stood at the corner of Forbes and Murray Avenues, in the heart of Pittsburgh's Squirrel Hill neighborhood. Mere hours after the shooting at the Tree of Life Synagogue building, thousands of us swayed as one community as local teens led us in *havdallah*. This weekly Saturday ritual, which marks the transition out of Shabbat (the Jewish sacred day of rest) and into the week ahead, took on a new meaning as that fateful day drew to a close. Night had fallen and Shabbat was over but I was drained and exhausted; even this potent ritual couldn't create a separation from that morning. My system was still in shock and distress, and there was a palpable sense of collective confusion about "what's next?"

As the last notes of *havdallah* hung in the air, my beloved and I found ourselves ensconced, scooped up under the arms of a Black man. One arm around each of us, he seemed to be cradling us both as he tenderly assured us, "You're not alone...we're here with you...we've got you." As the crowd began to swirl around us, time stopped as we stood shoulder to shoulder, still and silent. And then time started moving again, our eyes met briefly, and he was gone.

We had never seen him before, and we've not seen him since, but his presence, the way he showed up so solidly, left a question mark on my heart: how can *I* be a better ally? How can *I* show up better in solidarity with other communities in pain? How can I do a better job of loving, even those who I've never met, those I might never see again?

Memories of that evening often conjure the Talmud teaching "*Kol Yisrael aravim zeh l'zeh.*" One common understanding of this text is that "all Jewish people are responsible for one another." However, my experience that evening invited me to receive this wisdom in a more expansive way. If the name "Yisrael" is given to the one who wrestled with G-d, this can be read as follows: Each one who wrestles with *What has been/What is /What will be* bears responsibility for all others who also wrestle.

On that day I felt the strength and support from others who showed up for us, and there have certainly been other times where I have been isolated in my struggle. At the same time, I am proud of the times when I've been present for others in solidarity, and regretful when I haven't made it my priority to do so. This awareness made me realise that some days we *need* allies and some days we *are* allies. Perhaps social justice movements are called "movements" not just for the ways in which they move us toward a better world but also for the ways in which our position moves within them. What, then, does it mean to be an ally? And when is the right time to show up?

In order to approach the question, I've realized that we first need to understand what it means to be an ally? The world ally comes from the Latin word "ligare" which means "to be bound together" (like the word "obligate"). In some ways, it seems ironic that "allyship" is such a popular concept while American culture teaches us that we aren't obligated to anyone but ourselves, that our individual experiences come first and foremost.

This paradox made me wonder why the emphasis on individuality remains treasured in American society? Who benefits when we move through the world in that way, prizing our independence above all else? After consideration, I could only conclude that this societal norm serves those already in power, for when we act as though we're separate from one another, it causes us to forget that we're all connected. Systems of oppression thrive on our disconnection from one another in a way that invites those who hold power to tighten their grip.

White culture teaches us that the right thing to do is "answer the call" or to "respond to the needs of others", a dynamic which is predicated upon those in power defining both the problem and the terms of our action, affording those in power ongoing control. That same culture reinforces hierarchical models which place leaders at the top, in positions of power, a structure which fundamentally forgoes the strength of interconnection born out of cooperative leadership.

Never has this been more evident to me than in 2016 when I spent just a few days at Standing Rock. I had answered a clergy call while also curious about the power dynamic and how I might find my place. After all, I am a Person of Color but I am not Indigenous to this land and so I was clear that it was not my place to assert my leadership but rather to arrive as a guest and ally, there to support those who were leading the movement. To be honest, it was tricky to navigate as a newcomer, curbing the instinct of saviorism while also not wanting to put the onus on Indigenous leaders to teach me how to be or what to do. Almost immediately, I felt the tension of being an ally. It was unfamiliar territory in a culture which defaults to the binary, teaching us that we are either leaders or followers. I found myself bouncing between areas and projects, appealing to other allies for guidance amidst a landscape so unfamiliar. It dawned on me that my duty was to learn how to be an ally by actively trying to be an ally, learning to sit with the messiness and the discomfort of making mistakes, of working to mend relationships and of moving on even stronger for having done so.

When we begin to unlearn and relearn how to relate, we become more available to show up fully, to receive feedback, to unlearn and integrate. In doing so, we naturally begin to bind ourselves to one another, not only in an occasional act of resistance, but as an ongoing necessity of our liberation. For when we allow ourselves to be bound to one another, responsible to/for one another, we move beyond the kind of hierarchical systems which keep us in place and, paradoxically, our individual actions beget collective action. When we begin with the premise that none of us is free unless all of us are free, we work toward alignment where our actions are guided by the balance between individual benefit and collective good.

This worldview makes me think that perhaps "ally" is better understood as a verb, an action, than as a noun. To ally, then, is a pursuit without a destination or conclusion and the practice of allyship becomes an exercise in deep listening and discernment, with space for movement between leadership and followership, and always channeled through presence and heartfelt action. It is a spiritual practice guiding how we are with one another, imploring us to avail ourselves to those who are wrestling, not to save them but to be by their side.

On that late October day in 2018, that lesson was imprinted on my being: arms, unfamiliar yet safe, extending themselves in comfort and solidarity. In the meeting of our eyes, we were reminded that *Kol Yisrael aravim zeh l'zeh,* we need not wrestle alone. If only we let ourselves be bound together, we can share the burden of the struggle.

Be an Ally or Stand in Solidarity? An Omer Journey

Rabbi Ellen Lippmann

A slave and a child are sitting in a boat, waiting for a woman to join them. In many Talmudic passages, a slave, a woman, a child are considered "less than": lower in status or less educated or less capable. They are sometimes but not always in the same boat. Today let them stand for all who are seen as "less-than": people to be aided but who are not given full rights.

My question, as I write at the beginning of the month of Adar in the year 5781 or 2021, is where am I sitting? Am I the woman the slave and child are waiting for? That question will take me through Purim to Passover and the journey to Sinai beyond.

I know myself to be a white Ashkenazi Jewish lesbian cisgender woman rabbi. Except in the Biblical mythical sense I have never been a slave, though I have always understood that "You shall not wrong a stranger or oppress him, for you were strangers in the land of Egypt" (Exodus 22:20). In the Torah story, we were in fact strangers, and we were slaves to a cruel Pharaoh. For this reason, my interest in aid, allyship, and solidarity as described below most often refers to African-Americans, the people whose ancestors were slaves in this land and whose ongoing abuse at the hands of white

Americans is increasingly well documented. As I contemplate these questions, I imagine my peers, white Ashkenazi Jewish women, as a primary audience, but not the only one.

Because of the repetition in Torah and during annual Passover seders of the teaching about kindness to strangers, I came early to understand that I needed to offer assistance to "strangers," people I understood to be "not me." I gave *tzedakah* and still do regularly. I donated time and goods when asked and when possible. I was a reasonably good person, but not yet an ally.

What is An Ally?

Let's return to that boat. At this moment there are only a slave and a child in the boat. Let's say they are in that boat because they are fleeing to freedom. You are reading this soon after Passover seders when we retold the tale of our ancestors moving from freedom at the Red Sea to receiving Torah on Sinai, from slavery to imagining freedom and a better world.

Say the slave in the boat is African-American. It might be 1850 and they are urgently fleeing a plantation in the American south. Or it could be 1930 and, fearful of the ongoing violence of Jim Crow, this descendant of slaves flees as part of the Great Migration. Or it *is* 2021 and the slave has had enough of the deprivations of Northern liberals and the endless violence by police.

An ally in 2021 will have helped find the boat, ensured that it is seaworthy and has oars and life jackets, collected warm and waterproof clothing for the slave and child, has gathered donations of money sufficient to last several months in the place they are heading, and has brought a small crowd of the donors to the pier to see them safely off. Then the ally turns to her friends and says, "Let's go get coffee." And they do, and they return home to safety and warmth. It feels good to be an ally. You really helped.

On any number of occasions you would have found me at that coffee shop, sharing those good warm feelings with the other allies. And this kind of allyship *is* often really useful.

But something is missing, something that when realized will turn an ally into someone who acts in solidarity. The ally is removed, is not part of the story, will never get into that boat.

What is Solidarity?

Merriam-Webster says solidarity is "unity (as of a group or class) that produces or is based on community of interests, objectives, and standards."

Activist, writer, and teacher Eric Ward said that "solidarity that seems to be without a clear and identified self-interest is paternalism instead. Really [it] means skin in the game." He meant, I think, that we allies must wake up to a new reality in which we do not just try to bestow a freer, more just, humane world upon people seen as lesser, like the slave, woman and child in the Talmud. Now we begin to open our eyes to the reality that we too need that new world so that we ourselves can be fully human. The path toward that awakening is not easy. But neither are the limits of the privilege that we white Jews embrace unwittingly.

Sadly, sometimes the recognition of "skin in the game" emerges from fear or threat. A gunman attacks a synagogue, white nationalists march in Charlottesville, Jews are attacked in and near New York City, and a terrorist at the U.S. Capitol wears a "Camp Auschwitz" t-shirt. Now I am under the threat of attack that helps me awake to the reality of Black and brown Americans who are always subtly or overtly under attack, Black women especially, Black transwomen especially, whose lives are always in danger. But if I only see it that way, I may also cut off a new chance at solidarity. As Carin Mrotz wrote recently, "By positioning ourselves only as allies in fighting white supremacy, we'd erased the ways white supremacy directly targets us as Jews. We'd allowed our coalition partners to ignore Black Jews, Jews of color, and working-class Jews. We'd failed to understand our community as stakeholders and turned ourselves into saviors rather than co-conspirators. We'd also left our movement partners unprepared to support us when we needed it."[5]

---

5 Mrotz, Carin, 2021. "After the Insurrection Fighting Antisemitism Is a Critical Piece of a Racial Justice Agenda," *The Forge.* (February 15). Available from https://forgeorganizing.org/article/fighting-antisemitism-critical-piece-racial-justice-agenda (Accessed February 15, 2021).

Suddenly we white Jews find ourselves in a new or not-yet-recognized situation. In a recent article in *Religion News*, writer Yonat Shimron noted that the "the challenge for white American Jews is to understand that they can be both targets of white supremacy, and, at the same time, an accessory to it. 'It's both/and,' said April Baskin, a Black Jewish activist. 'We can both be targeted by anti-Semitism and also be benefitting from racism at the same time.'"[6]

As a Jew whose German immigrant ancestors were seen in 1850 as dark and foreign and dangerous, in 2021 it is completely clear that I am a white person to anyone who sees me on the street. And there my danger recedes.

But if I can listen well to those whose stories I do not know, whose fears and hopes I can learn to know, and can gather the courage to ask for attention to my stories as well, then I can begin to realize that all of our humanity is diminished by injustice to any of us. I can learn to feel the hurt, the pain, not to begin to do, to act, but to begin to let those feelings enter my heart. I can let go of my fear of being wrong, of being uncomfortable, and try to see with newly opened eyes what may need doing. I stop doing *for* others and do *with* others, because we are in some basic way in the same

---

6 Shimron, Yonat. 2021. "American Jews Are Taking a Hard Look at Racism in Their Midst.' *Religion News Service.* (February 12). Available from https://religionnews.com/2021/02/12/american-jews-are-taking-a-hard-look-at-racism-in-their-midst/ (Accessed February 12, 2021).

boat. If I can risk exposing my heart, my humanity, we can move forward together.

Moving forward together is often seen as a threat by those who hold onto their power ever more tightly when they fear the strength of our unity, and its power. Regular attempts are made to divide Jews and Blacks, for instance, but similar attempts have always ensued in the face of solidarity.

In the 1977 Combahee River Collective Statement, a group of powerful Black feminists said, "We believe that the most profound and potentially most radical politics come directly out of our own identity, as opposed to working to end somebody else's oppression. In the case of Black women this is a particularly repugnant, dangerous, threatening, and therefore revolutionary concept because it is obvious from looking at all the political movements that have preceded us that anyone is more worthy of liberation than ourselves. We reject pedestals, queenhood, and walking ten paces behind. To be recognized as human, levelly human, is enough."[7]

"To be recognized as human is enough." Should that not be our goal at all times? Yet there is sacrifice in getting there. I as a white Jewish woman must also give up the pedestals, the false elevation, even the subservience or protection

---

7 BlackPast, B. (2012, 1977) *The Combahee River Collective Statement.* (November 16). Retrieved from https://www.blackpast.org/african-american-history/combahee-river-collective-statement-1977/

that have kept me safe. How can I be safe when the women who might become my sisters are never safe? How can we sail to safety together?

My friend Imani Chapman, an Afro-Latina Jew, has written, "Solidarity extends beyond simple empathy, which means "feeling with." Solidarity emerges from common interest... Many of us become overwhelmed by the learning process of simply recognizing injustice and are fatigued before approaching the stage of undoing injustice. We need the staying power—garnered from relationships, rest, and ritual—that keep us from turning on one another and keep us moving together."[8]

A slave and a child are sitting in a boat. Do I dare to join them? I imagine that I have joined the slave and the child because I have come to recognize that I cannot just donate to the boat or stand on the pier if, like them, I am to get to freedom, to the place where all are seen as fully human.[9] I frankly still struggle, fear what I will give up to sit there. How many of my friends think me crazy? How many will condemn me when the going gets rough? I sense what I may gain, yearn for it, but there is still far to go. With tense anticipation, and in tentative solidarity, I sit in the

---

8 From an essay in a soon-to-be-published Torah commentary.
9 This might be the "the land that I will show you" noted in Genesis 12:1 where G-d promises this possibility to Abraham as G-d tells Abraham to "get going." Or it might be Mt. Sinai, where G-d offers Moses and the freed slaves a divine vision for a better world.

boat, ready to listen to the slave and the child, ready to share my story as part of the sea on which we sail.

Are you coming?

Allyship: When the Answer is the Question

Rabbi Maharat Rori Picker Neiss

Oftentimes the most significant moments of allyship emerge when one first takes the time to pause, to notice, to question, and to open one's heart for the response. Because it is only when we see people, *truly* see people, and allow ourselves to bear witness to their stories, only then can we then take our first steps alongside them on their journey towards liberation.

The Torah teaches us this lesson again and again, but it is perhaps best exemplified in the origin stories of two of the great heroes of the Jewish tradition: Moses and King David. These two individuals play crucial roles in the salvation of the Israelite people: the former in their redemption from unfathomable oppression and the latter in their establishment as a united people in their promised land. Yet, while each served as a military leader and a symbol of strength, their personal journeys begin in far more unassuming ways: with a question.

Moses is famously called by G-d in the story of the burning bush. The text states

> Now Moses, tending the flock of his father-in-law Jethro, the priest of Midian, drove the flock into the wilderness, and came to Horeb, the mountain of G-d. An

94

angel of the Lord appeared to him in a blazing fire out of a bush. He gazed, and there was a bush all aflame, yet the bush was not consumed. Moses said, "I must turn aside to look at this marvelous sight; why doesn't the bush burn up?" When the Lord saw that he had turned aside to look, G-d called to him out of the bush: "Moses! Moses!" He answered, "Here I am." (Exodus 3:1-4)

Nachmanides, the leading medieval Jewish scholar in Catalonia, notices the discrepancy between the beginning of the story when an angel appears to Moses and its climax when it is the Lord who speaks directly to Moses. He asserts that, in fact, G-d was always present with the burning bush, but that Moses could not behold the presence of G-d until he had prepared his heart to do so. Only once he opened his heart to bear witness to the wonder he beheld could he experience G-d and hear the call.

Even more striking in this text is that the story is ambiguous whether the call is intended from the outset exclusively for Moses. Indeed, it is only when the Lord sees that Moses had turned aside that the Lord calls out to Moses.

We can then read this as a story in which G-d has put out an open call, and Moses is the first to respond. Moreover, his response itself is noteworthy. Moses sees something that is outside of his lived experience. He actively stops, takes the time to turn aside to look more closely, asks a question to demonstrate his authentic desire to know more, and then opens his heart to receive a response. G-d sees this as rendering him worthy of leadership. This is what is necessary to be able to guide the people towards freedom.

We are introduced to a similar concept in the story of King David, although in a tale that predates his birth as it introduces his grandparents: the encounter of Boaz and Ruth. Boaz, the Rabbis teach us, is from a lineage of leadership. According to the Midrash, the Rabbinic exegesis, his father was Nachshon ben Aminadav, the brother in law of Aaron, himself the brother of Moses, and the first one to walk into the Sea of Reeds, so confident in his trust of G-d even before the sea began to split. Even without this interpretive layer, we can see in the text of the Book of Ruth that he is a wealthy man who owns fields, oversees workers, and earns the respect of the townspeople of his city. And it is for all those reasons that it is striking when, in the story, he sees a woman gleaning from his fields and asks about her. We as the reader of the story have to assume that as a man of significant means, Boaz is accustomed to seeing the poor walk through his fields in the hope of picking up some of the crop dropped by one of his workers. Indeed, we might even be surprised that he is in the fields at all, instead of leaving this task to the managers.

Unlike in the story of Moses, what Boaz sees is not miraculous or incongruous. Nevertheless, he turns aside to see that which surrounds him, even that which might surround him every day. He asks a question about it, wanting to know more about this woman. Then, he prepares himself for a response. He learns that she is a foreigner. He learns that she is related to Naomi. Knowing all that, he knows that she is an outsider, without resources or means, without the protection of a husband who died or wealth that was lost. He knows that she is vulnerable. And once knowing her story, he can begin to offer support.

It is significant that this is recorded as the lineage of King David: the union of the one who has experienced oppression together with the one who stopped to see it. This intersection, the Torah wants us to know, is where leadership must stand.

For both Moses and for Boaz, the responses to their questions led to action, but their path to liberation nevertheless started with a question and with a willingness to be moved by the answers.

The role of an ally might seem daunting at times. The problems people face might be large, the systems that perpetuate injustice run deep, and the suffering can be overwhelming. Yet, it is not the role of an ally to have the answers. People determine their own paths to liberation. It is the role of the ally to see, to recognize, to seek to learn, and to listen.

Indeed it is only when these two individuals, Moses and Boaz, connected to those suffering but not a part of those suffering, prepared themselves to open their hearts and recognize their calling

that the journey to liberation began for the entire
people.

On Chosenness As Allyship: Our Inheritance As Children of Abraham

Rabbi Michelle Dardashti

> *"I know, I know. We are Your chosen people. But once in a while, can't You choose someone else?"* Tevye, the Milkman (Fiddler on the Roof, 1971 Film).

The meanings and implications of Jewish chosenness have been contemplated and contested throughout the centuries. What's the nature of Jewish exceptionalism as derived from the Hebrew Bible? What is it exactly for which the Jewish people have been singled out: for favor or for suffering?

Tevye's aggrieved reflection that the Jewish people were seemingly chosen for exceptional suffering does find expression in our sacred texts, but so do notions of our having been chosen to dominate, care and intervene. In fact, all four of these ideas are all present within stories about Abraham, the individual chosen to father the Jewish people; suffering is not the most pronounced, but merely the final one we see. This essay glances back at each of these stories, attempting to understand how they relate to one another and to how we, Abraham's progeny, are meant to relate to the world.

The biblical account of Abram (before he is renamed Abraham) begins in Genesis Chapter 12, with his receipt of a call from G-d to leave his home for a new land and a new destiny: "I will make of you a great nation. And I will bless you; I will make your name great, and you shall be a blessing." Inspired by these promises, Abram goes forth. In so doing, he teaches us lessons about what it means to be great and what it looks like to be a blessing.

Abram's first act of greatness comes through his heroic intervention in a war between two feuding groups of tribes: he rescues kings, returns possessions and redeems captives. In this story, found in Genesis 14, Abram shows up as not merely an ally, but an accomplice. He gets his hands dirty and puts his body on the line in service of others. While the capture of his nephew Lot seems to be the impetus for Abram's engagement in this war, it's clear that Abram is in deep relationship with others in the region and involved in the feud. The text names three Amorites with whom Abram is "*baalei brit.*" These words literally mean "owners of covenant," but practically speaking, it means they were allies. Abram comes through for his kinsman, Lot, *and* for his allies; thus, he is a blessing.

Later, in Chapter 18, our patriarch pleads on behalf of people of Sodom and Gomorrah; he bargains relentlessly for G-d to mitigate the severity of the decree against these cities, asking: "Will you sweep away the innocent, along with the guilty? ... Shall not the Judge of all the earth deal justly?" Here, while Abraham may not be an accomplice, he is a remarkable upstander and it is clear that G-d wants and expects him to play this role. The Torah conveys that G-d feels compelled to share with Abraham what is about to befall the sinful cities: "Shall I hide from Abraham what I am about to do, since Abraham is to become a great and populous nation and all the nations of the earth are to bless themselves by him? For I have singled him out, that he may instruct his children and his posterity to keep the way of the LORD by doing what is just and right..." This text makes explicit that, for G-d, becoming great and being a blessing are synonymous with being an ally; being chosen ("singled out") is about doing what is just and right.

But between these two stories, of our protagonist as courageous ally-accomplice and then as steadfast ally-upstander, something deeply disappointing happens. One wonders if G-d underscores the purpose of election as about increasing the doing of "what is just and right" because Abraham does something so very wrong just prior.

In Chapter 16, despairing of her barrenness in the face of G-d's promise to make his descendants number the stars, Abram's wife, Sarai, resolves to supply herself and Abram with progeny "through her handmaiden, Hagar." Once Hagar becomes pregnant by Abram, however, Sarai is consumed by jealousy. She abuses Hagar and Abram sanctions the abuse; he is at best a bystander and at worst an enabler. The 12th century sage,

Ramban (Rabbi Moses ben Nahman), condemns our ancestors' behavior and I believe G-d does as well. When Abram fails to be an ally, G-d steps in.

Hagar flees Sarai's abuse and an angel of G-d finds her and promises her, too, numerous descendants. The angel tells her to return to the tent of Abram and Sarai, assured of this promise and knowing that G-d has witnessed her suffering. Commentators, including Ramban, view the Israelites' travails as strangers in Egypt centuries later, as retribution for the suffering inflicted upon Hagar, who was Egyptian and whose name is connected to the word for stranger.

What transpires in Chapter 16 results in our ancestors' names, and perhaps the destiny of their descendants, being forever changed.

Their harsh treatment of Hagar indicates to G-d that Abram and Sarai have misunderstood G-d's intent through their chosenness. In Chapter 17, therefore, G-d adds a *heh* (Hebrew "H" sound) to their names, making them Abraham and Sarah, reflecting a desire for them to be the patriarch and matriarch of "*many* nations" (*hamon goyim*) and not concerned only with the fate of their distinct line. Abraham's internalization of this expanded understanding of his mandate might account for his zeal in arguing on behalf of Sodom and Gomorrah. Sarah, however, isn't able to broaden her gaze; once she bears Isaac, in Chapter 21, she cannot find room in her tent, or heart, for Hagar and Ishmael.

The story of Abraham's near sacrifice of Isaac, in Chapter 22, follows closely on the heels of

Abraham and Sarah's banishment of Hagar and Ishmael in Chapter 21. Based on striking linguistic parallels between the two stories, I believe that Abraham is tested through the command to sacrifice Isaac as a consequence of what Hagar and Ishmael were made to endure.

G-d determines that the only way to ensure that Avraham and Sarah feel the sting of their excess particularism, is to have them suffer similarly to Hagar and Ishmael. While both Isaac and Abraham physically survive "the test," Sarah does not; the 11th century sage, Rashi, maintains that upon learning that Abraham set off to sacrifice Isaac, her soul promptly left her body. The text also reflects that the relationship between Abraham and Isaac is never the same again.

The adjacent chapters about Abraham and his sons, in which both nearly die by their father's hand, one by banishment, the other by slaughter, offer a warning: when chosenness seems to demand dominance or discrimination, chosenness manifesting as suffering follows. While I am not implying that Jewish suffering throughout Jewish history can be attributed to failing to be good allies, I am suggesting that our behavior as oppressors will never end well for us. A posture toward the world that reflects deep interconnectedness with others is what G-d intends for the Jewish people.

It is fitting that we read Chapters 21 and 22 of Genesis on Rosh HaShanah, the Birthday of the World and not the Birthday of the Jewish people.

Rosh HaShanah is the universalist start to the Jewish year, while Passover, which falls in month one on the Jewish calendar, is our particularist beginning. These stories of the internal family dynamics, which tear Abraham's tent apart, teach us how *not* to understand our chosenness. Rosh HaShanah, marking a universal moment of celebration, is the perfect antidote to interpreting chosenness as permission to inflict suffering upon others.

The stories of Abraham, taken together, suggest that being chosen for suffering is not an inevitability. As Jews, we must consistently strive to draw out the *"heh,"* the letter that represents expansion and G-dliness, in our name and self-understanding. We must choose to embrace chosenness as a call toward involvement, intervention and deep care for all families of the earth.

No, G-d can't choose someone else. Meaningful allyship is our inheritance.

From Avdut to Cherut: Changing Ourselves to Change the World

Rabbi Lauren Tuchman

One of the central motifs in the Pesach seder is our journey from degradation to praise, from narrowness to expansiveness, from slavery to freedom. We are now *b'midbar*, in the wilderness, making our way to Sinai, to covenant and to radical collectivity. We were all at Sinai, every Jewish soul past, present and future, beyond the limitations of time and space to receive Torah. We heard the aleph in anochi, I, all together and separately in a way we could understand. This is why, as we learn repeatedly in rabbinic tradition, the Torah has seventy faces, infinite interpretive possibilities. G-d desires all of us to receive Torah, to be met by Torah and to be in relationship with these sacred instructions, all the while knowing that our relationships with that instruction, Torah in its broadest definition, are as varied as we are.

This sounds quite lofty and abstract: being met by the Divine? Radical relationship? How are we, how am I, supposed to live that out if I am someone who has been cast aside, wounded by that Torah that I am told is a Torat Chayyim, a life-giving Torah? In a world in which the examples of religious leaders misusing, abusing, and weaponizing Torah against those who are marginalized is legion and unfortunately always growing, or so it seems, thinking about allyship as a spiritual practice rings hollow. Knowing just how profound alienation from the religious community is for folks who have been and are now marginalized and knowing my own human limitations, how do I live out this aspirational practice authentically?

In his book *Changing the World from the Inside Out,* my teacher Rabbi David Jaffe challenges us to encounter the self through deeply-rooted Jewish spiritual and ethical practice as a means of building a resilient inner core, which anchors us in a profoundly uncertain and destabilizing world. We cannot change the world, Rabbi Jaffe claims, if we aren't working on internal change.

Too often, allyship becomes performative: a title we ascribe to ourselves and not a posture of profound humility we earn over time through authentic partnership, radical listening and embracing the notion, which is anathema in a Western cultural context utterly obsessed with knowledge gathering and action, that we in fact don't know everything. We have so much to learn from others we too often ignore because, though we may not admit this to ourselves, we fall into the trap of assuming that our educational attainments, or class, or our race, or our ability status allows us to have an objective view on what others need, those who are "less fortunate." They don't have all of the information they need to make impactful decisions for their lives and communities. Radical listening and accepting just how little we know allows us to turn this notion on its head. We are aware that we hold a piece of the tapestry of the human experience. We also know that ours is not the finishing piece of the puzzle. So much Torah has yet to be revealed to us. Or, perhaps, G-d is desperately trying to make known to us through encounters and events in our lives that Torah which we refuse to uncover because it shakes us, challenges us, asks us to let go of biases we may desperately wish we didn't hold because we are good people after all. I believe that we have unfortunately ascribed a moral judgement to the inevitability of holding unconscious negative bias. We have all grown up in cultural contexts that had embedded within them ideas about people of all sorts. Messaging that we receive is so subconscious that it takes years of conscious unlearning and relearning to rewire our neural pathways. Spiritual practice is not about the destination. Though we are heading towards a mountaintop moment, ours is a spirituality rooted in the sanctification of the everyday. As we unlearn, we relearn. None of us is free of unconscious negative bias. Our task as spiritual practitioners is to deepen our inner awareness so that we show up with the most authenticity we can in our external reality.

I fear that we have become so focused on wokeness, on knowing the right language, reading the right books, hearing the right speakers that we are neglecting the reality that we are constantly a work in progress. G-d is infinite, we are finite. If we don't allow ourselves to learn not merely to learn but also to put our learning into action, we will forever be caught in the self-defeating trap of fearing doing the wrong thing so much that we become frozen, unable to act at all.

With gentleness and compassion, Rabbi Jaffe invites us to explore our growing edges through Mussar and the teachings of Rabbi Nachman of Breslov. A particularly impactful piece of his work for me is his teachings about *bitachon*, trust. There is no doubt that *bitachon* is a tough bridge to cross. Social change and good allyship is about action, about using my voice, my resources to stand alongside communities who are too often silenced. Isn't *bitachon* a passive act? In fact, *bitachon* is precisely the opposite. Trusting that I hold what is mine to hold and that I am able to be in a radical collaborative relationship with others allows me to remember, always, that I am part of that which is greater than myself. Allyship is not about the ego or escapism. Rather, it is about doing my own work through daily cheshbon hanefesh—soul accounting or another spiritual discipline so that I can show up most humbly in my external work. If my internal reality is consumed by a ceaseless need for self-gratification, I am stuck in an *avdut* consciousness. I have not made that journey as we are invited to during the seder from narrowness to expansiveness. I know both from personal experience and from the experiences of others that those who are not working on themselves but are seeking some external validation through allyship are some of the greatest impediments to meaningful social transformation. Human beings are not revolution objects, not canvases on which we thrust our baggage. If I am to be an ally in the deepest sense, I must never forget that I, being created in the Image of G-d, am radically meeting another being created in G-d's image, as inherently beloved as I am. Giving myself space to grow, to try something and not succeed, to learn from my mistakes allows the spiritual practice of allyship to be made that much more manifest. As the Psalmist teaches in Psalms 16:8, I keep the Divine before me, always. It is not upon me, as we learn in Perkei Avot to complete the work, but I am neither free to desist from it. Just as Shabbat is a container for the world as it should be, allowing us to taste a moment of redemption each week, so, too, is allyship a sacred container, allowing us to radically encounter the other and the self, remembering, always, that we are all interconnected one with another.

"I am Joseph.
You are Joseph."

Rabbi Roderick Young

Midrash! It is the most wonderful invention of the rabbis of old. Its root meaning is "to search out." And that's what the rabbis did. From the gaps, the difficulties, the puzzles and the silences of the Biblical text they ferreted out stories to flesh out the Holy details. Midrash is imagination, mental fireworks, a revealing of the divine.

Consider that fascinating and high maintenance character, Joseph. Joseph irritatingly told his brothers that he had dreamed that sheaves of corn and then the sun, moon and stars were bowing down before him. He left no-one in any doubt that it was his family who would bow down before him! That boy must have been a joy to live with...

Shortly after these dreams, Joseph's father sent him to check on his brothers in the fields where they were pasturing their sheep. But on the way to the fields, the dreamer gets lost and we read this strange little verse: "A man came upon him wandering in the fields. The man asked him, 'What are you looking for?'" (Genesis 37: 15). The man gives him directions and Joseph goes on his way.

Hello? Excuse me? But who, exactly, is this man? He walks into the text, says a couple of lines and then he disappears from the pages of history.

Time to consult a Torah Detective! So I turn to one of the best, the Kotzker Rebbe, an outstanding 19th century Hasidic leader. And what does the Kotzker Rebbe make of this mysterious incident? He tells me that the man was an angel who taught Joseph that we have to seek ourselves. "Yeah, yeah" I grumble, "Here he goes with that Know Thyself shtick again." Well, I suppose I'll just have to solve the mystery myself.

So, Mr. Kotzker Rebbe, this is what I know. The man was an angel. He had broad shoulders, shining black hair and dancing green eyes. He said to Joseph: "Nu, Yossele, want to share a dream or two?" And the two of them ran hand in hand into the Midbar Kadesh where they lived together for 20 years, eating mangoes, studying the Torah and holding each other tightly as the mauve sun sank into the sand. After 20 years Joseph knew it was time to return to the story, and so they parted on the sand, each walking in the opposite direction, carrying only a kiss given by the other. Joseph walked to Egypt and with a sigh took up the narrative; but, try as he might, he never could get interested in Mrs. Potiphar.

"OK, Mr. Kotzker Rebbe," I said, "how come you never tell that part of the story?" Of course, I didn't expect an answer. So I must admit I was surprised when a wheezy voice whispered into my ear: "Didn't I tell you that you must seek yourself? And didn't you look and find that you, too, are between the lines of the Holy Torah?" I don't tell too many people this. After all, who would believe that the Kotzker Rebbe taught me to write queer midrash?

After many years of living in Egypt Joseph becomes the grand panjandrum, second only to Pharaoh himself. Forced out of Canaan by a famine, his brothers come to Egypt to plead for food and they don't recognise the kohl-eyed, gold covered royal as their annoying little brother. Joseph, the mighty ruler, puts them through the wringer, accusing them of theft and threatening to keep the youngest brother as a slave.

But eventually Joseph cracks. His sobs and tears fill the palace. He faces his brothers and says: "I am Joseph." Remember the Kotzker Rebbe? Well, Joseph has sought himself. He now knows who he is and can name himself to the world. He has become the human who G-d created him to be. And in fact he says more than just his name. He says: "I am Joseph. Is my father still well?" First he tells the world who he is and immediately he then asks, with true care, after another person.

Joseph teaches us that to be an ally to another human we must first know ourselves. We must know ourselves in all our imperfections, in all our weaknesses and in all our strengths. We must try to be ruthlessly honest with ourselves and about ourselves. When we understand our own pain and our own joy then we can all the more easily empathise with other people who may not be walking the same path as us. We become good allies when we offer unconditional help from a place of honesty that recognises our differences and yet upholds our common humanity.

Hundreds of years after Joseph, in the desert between Egypt and Israel, Aaron, the brother of Moses, watched in silent horror as G-d struck down his eldest sons. Midrash can hear his thoughts: "My sons, my two beautiful boys. Back in Egypt, on our last night in our old home, as the sons of the Egyptians died all around us and the keening of their mothers echoed up and down the streets, we were protected by the blood on the door. The Angel of Death passed over the house. But as he swooped by I thought I heard a feather scrape the roof. And now, after all these years he has come suddenly to take my sons. Could you not have forgiven them? Could it not have been Passover again?"

In a terrible turn of the wheel Aaron experiences the same unspeakable pain as the Egyptians. Throughout the Torah we are continually told to treat the strangers amongst us with kindness and justice, because we were strangers in Egypt. To have empathy is a divine commandment, so to be an ally to another human is a divine commandment. We learn to be allies with humans who may be different from us though the shared joy of Joseph. We learn to be allies with those who may be different from us through the shared grief of Aaron.

In 384 C.E. the Roman senator Symmachus, a pagan, wrote to the Christian Emperor Valentinian II: "It is reasonable that whatever each of us worships is really to be considered one and the same. We gaze up at the same stars, the sky covers us all, the same universe compasses us. What does it matter what practical system we adopt in our search for the truth? Not by one avenue only can we arrive at so tremendous a secret."

The essence of humanity is to look over at the avenue being trodden by someone else and, no matter how different they are to us in race, religion, gender, sexuality, age or experience, to say to them: "How can I be a support to you?"

We can't walk the same path as everyone else, but we can stretch out our hands and raise our voices. And if someone doesn't reach a hand back towards us immediately, well, we know that there are stories of pain and joy in the silence and some day we may be privileged to hear them.

Allyship as Imagination and Empathy

Rabbi Deborah Waxman, Ph.D.

Rabbi Yochanan ben Zakkai taught:

> If you have a sapling in your hand and someone tells you the Messiah has arrived, first plant the sapling and then go out to welcome the Messiah (Avot d'Rabbi Natan 31b).

Rabbi Yochanan ben Zakkai had a profound capacity to imagine the future, even in the darkest moments of his own life and that of his people. Despairing at the zeal of the rebels in Jerusalem as the Second Temple was threatened in 73 CE, he smuggled himself out of the city in a coffin and convinced the conquering Roman army to allow him to establish a center of Jewish learning in the Galilee, planting the seeds for rabbinic Judaism that would flourish for millennia. Facing devastation, both personal and communal, he seeded a vital future.

Rabbi Yochanan ben Zakkai is a powerful model for being an ally. Allyship is an exercise of imagination and empathy. It is an investment in a future we may not live to see. Allyship does not perpetuate the status quo but embraces change: sometimes incremental, sometimes radical. It presumes that change is life-affirming, both individually and collectively. Taking action as an ally brings to life a commitment that someone who does not look or act like me has equal value and is worth my time and energy to champion.

This apocryphal teaching attributed to Rabbi Yochanan ben Zakkai is a powerful text in support of allyship. At its core is a vision of a redeemed world brought by the Messiah, a world where inequality and iniquity is swept away and justice prevails. Yochanan ben Zakkai surely believed in such a Messiah. And he was, it seems, a pragmatist. This teaching suggests that we ordinary folk have work to do before, and during, and even after the Messiah comes.

It is likely not accidental that the work specified in this text is planting rather than other common tasks of the time. Our ancestors were nomads who pined for a "land of milk and honey" in their wanderings, and then became farmers in a region with extreme limitations on water. Agriculture sits at the intersection of the human and the natural. We insert ourselves into that which might happen naturally to clear and fertilize, plant and prune, tend and harvest. So too with justice. Yochanan ben Zakkai advances a messianic vision but does not counsel passivity. The Messiah will not solve every problem or meet every need. We will, we must play a role in that "world to come": especially in bringing it about. As allies, we can insert ourselves into that which seems "natural," very often a status quo that replicates what always has been, to nurture it toward a richer, more bountiful reality that is more inclusive and just.

The focus on a sapling is also particularly powerful. Judaism teaches that planting trees in particular is an investment in the future. The Babylonian Talmud (Taanit 23a) tells the story of Honi the Circle Maker, who was walking along a road and saw a man planting a carob sapling.

> Ḥoni said to him: "This tree, after how many years will it bear fruit?" The man said to him: "It will not produce fruit until seventy years have passed." Ḥoni said to him: "Is it obvious to you that you will live seventy years, that you expect to benefit from this tree?" He said to him: "[I] found a world full of carob trees. Just as my ancestors planted for me, I too am planting for my descendants."

The story continues that Honi then fell asleep nearby and, like a Jewish Rip van Winkle, lay hidden and slept for 70 years. When he awoke, he encountered a man harvesting fruit from the now mature tree. When he inquired, Honi learned that the harvester was the grateful son of the planter.

Allyship so often is an act of faith, a way to carefully plant and grow the future we want to see, with the keen awareness that that future can, even should, look profoundly different from the present, and hopefully it will be a future of abundance and nourishment and justice for all. But it's not only about the future, it's also about right now. Allyship is an opportunity to bring a taste of the messianic era into the present moment through action. Standing up for someone on the margins, mentoring, hiring, promoting, championing BIPOC, people with disabilities, LGBTQIA individuals, folks from different socioeconomic and cultural backgrounds, and women, alter individual trajectories and transform cultural realities in real and meaningful ways. May we all imagine richly. May we all plant many trees, real and metaphorical. May we all tend and act in the most powerful and fruitful ways, for our own collective sake and for our descendants.

Storytelling as Allyship

Rabbi David M. Rosenberg

What kind of stories do we tell...

...about our own lives?
...about the lives of our families?
...about our communities?
...about the history of Jewish life in the US, Israel, Canada, the UK, Australia, South Africa...?
...about the history of the Jewish people?

Our world is full of stories about success, prowess, beauty, brilliance, and wealth. We can see all around us images of apparent happiness and accomplishment. The contemporary Jewish world often reflects a similar focus in our stories and images. The proverbial Jewish boy grows up to be a doctor or a Nobel prize-winning mathematician. I grew up with these stories and saw them as a faithful depiction of what the world is, or what it should be. Much of my career has been focused on success, brilliance, and accomplishment. When I served as a Hillel director, I saw my role as helping highly intelligent young people to succeed in university and beyond. Of course, many students struggled with emotional, physical, and economic challenges. Overall, the story remained the same: a story of success in the making.

When I came to a Jewish human services agency, I confronted a different reality: for many of the people I serve, life is not a straight path to accomplishment and happiness. The individuals and families that turn to my agency for services do so because they encounter challenges to success. Those challenges are real, not just for the people directly impacted but also for their broader community. I have found again and again, when I describe the work I do, that the person with whom I am conversing has experienced some of the same challenges in their immediate or extended family.

I have learned that our Jewish stories must reflect the lived reality of individuals and families who do not experience conventional success, who do not fit neatly into the various molds of "normalcy" and happiness that conventional narratives describe. Our stories must include those who experience pain and doubt, who wrestle with mental illness, who are challenged in their relationships with family and friends, who do not conform to expectations about sexuality and gender identity, who are unable to run a 100 yard dash, do their times tables, or read and respond to text messages. They and their realities must not be airbrushed away from our accounts. We must include the richness of those individuals and their realities not out of a sense of noblesse oblige or pity for those deemed "less fortunate," but out of a recognition that challenge and difference are part of the human condition and must be part of the Jewish story. How many people have denied the complexities of their *own* lived experience in order to conform to the expectations of a conventional story?

We are blessed with Jewish resources that can help us tell a truer and richer account of the Jewish and human condition.

The holiday of Passover commemorates the pain of slavery as well as the joy of liberation. The Mishnah (3rd century) instructs us that at the Seder one should retell the Exodus by "beginning with degradation (the tale of suffering) and ending with praise (the celebration of leaving Egypt" (Pesachim 10:4). Many commentators understand the seven weeks between Passover and Shavuot in a similar way, as a journey of spiritual growth from the degradation of Egypt to the glorious revelation of Torah at Mount Sinai. The story of Revelation is part of a broader narrative that includes the challenges of those who lived through it. It is tempting to imagine that all who stood at Sinai were models of physical ability and beauty, brilliant and happy. Yet a people that camped "as one person, with one heart" (Rashi on Exodus 19:2) included people with their unique strengths and challenges, sufferings, and questioning.

Perhaps the most powerful recognition that experiences of suffering and of difference must be part of the Jewish story comes from the prophet Isaiah. Describing the "servant of the Lord," a collective expression for the Jewish people in many parts of the book, the prophet teaches, "the many were appalled at them— So marred was their appearance, unlike that of human, form, beyond human semblance" (Isaiah 52:14).

The prophet continues:

Upon whom has the arm of the NAME been revealed?

For they have grown, by Divine favor, like a tree crown,

Like a tree trunk out of arid ground. They had no form or beauty, that we should look at them:

No charm, that we should find them pleasing.

They were despised, shunned by people,

Person of suffering, familiar with disease.

As one who hid their face from us,

They were despised, we held them of no account. (Isaiah 53:1-3)

The Jewish people that the prophet describes growing "like a tree crown" are the same people who "had no form or beauty," the same who were "despised" and "shunned."

Many readers focus on Isaiah 53 as an announcement of a glorious future. Yet this chapter also includes messages for the world which we actually inhabit. *We* can encounter this prophecy as a depiction of community and life as they really are. Our story includes and must include the experience of being despised, shunned, of suffering, and of being seen as less than human because we may not conform to conventional expectations. If being shunned has been part of one's own experience, such a story can be, in part at least, autobiographical. If one's own life has been one of personal success and public acclaim, then including the full range of human experience in the telling of the Jewish story becomes a form of allyship in storytelling.

Storytelling as allyship is a way to show regard for the full range of human experience in our families, communities, and people (as well as in our own lives!). It is a way to testify to the truth. It is a way to show regard to the rich range of individuals in our lives, communities, and people over all generations. And it is a way to bring the fullness of life and people into a future that moves from "degradation" to "praise."

On Allyship and Action

Rabbi Dara Lithwick

My Judaism is a welcoming tradition, an affirming tradition. It is one that recognizes the Divine spark in each and every one of us and calls on us to use our faculties, designed in the Divine image, to co-create a better world.

It is also a tradition of struggle, one that does not let us off the hook in terms of our obligations to each other. A necessary corollary, I think, of the understanding that we are all created *b'tzelem Elohim*, in the Divine image, is a responsibility for us to uphold the dignity and respect of all people and taking action in ways we can to support and advocate with groups experiencing marginalization and social injustice. To be allies to each other.

Finally, Judaism is also a tradition of much joy, where we celebrate creation in its diversity throughout the cycles of the year. It is a tradition where I feel so at home that ultimately, I decided in my thirties to study to become a rabbi.

I would not have followed this path if not for allyship.

Back in the mid-1990s, before Ellen DeGeneres "came out" on her television sitcom (a bit of a cultural turning point), I came out to my parents. I was about 19 years old. Many questions surfaced for me. Could I reconcile myself with myself? Could I still be Jewish? Raise a family? Be a part of the community?

The answers then were not so clear. My parents did not take my coming out well, and approached my former rabbi in Montreal, Rabbi Leigh Lerner, to see if he had any advice regarding how to, well, straighten me out.

Instead of finding names of conversion therapists, they walked out of the meeting with Rabbi Lerner having committed together to start a PFLAG (Parents and Friends of Lesbians and Gays) group at our Temple. It was a transformative moment both in my coming out process and in my Judaism. Rabbi Lerner's allyship, his unwavering support of me as a person, as a member of the community, his belief that I was just right the way I was and that I should be proud, helped bring my family around to acceptance and love. Through him, I was able to see my Judaism and my G-d as welcoming, loving, and powerfully relevant to any life challenges I faced. Rabbi Lerner showed me the power and import of allyship.

A few years before that, though, was when I first took in the necessity for us to stand up for each other's fundamental dignity and human rights. It was the first time that I recalled feeling the power of G-d, and of human capacity for both good and evil. I was sixteen years old on a trip called the March of the Living, to Poland and Israel. I was on a bus with youth from Canada as we toured old Jewish Krakow and met Jews struggling to rebuild Jewish life in Warsaw. We went to camps such as Majdanek and Auschwitz-Birkenau. Then, in Israel we welcomed newcomers, celebrated Yom Ha'atzma'ut and more.

With us was Anna Heilmann, a survivor of Majdanek and Auschwitz, who along with her sister and other Jewish women, was part of a plot to blow up Crematorium IV in October 1944 at Auschwitz-Birkenau. Anna's sister and three other women were captured and murdered two weeks before the camp was liberated. Yet their acts of resistance saved countless lives by making Crematorium IV unusable.

Anna's story and her love and courage has stayed with me. In a 1986 interview, fellow survivor Elie Wiesel said: "The opposite of love is not hate, its indifference. The opposite of beauty is not ugliness, its indifference. The opposite of faith is not heresy, its indifference. And the opposite of life is not death, but indifference..."

Rabbi Abraham Joshua Heschel, civil rights leader, added: "The opposite of good is not evil; the opposite of good is indifference. In a free society where terrible wrongs exist, some are guilty, but all are responsible."

In those formative years as a late teen I was lucky to have allies and role models that helped me affirm my own responsibility and voice and enabled me to be, well, me – a whole, integrated self.

Today, now, as a woman in my early 40s, I am grateful for the rights that I have and for the life that I am able to live. I stand on the shoulders of other activists and allies. I am grateful that I was able to marry my wife, my bashert, and that we were able to parent our children and be recognized in society, on forms at school, and at synagogue, as both being "parents."

Just as I have benefitted from allyship, it is upon me to "ally up," to stand up and support friends and colleagues and community members and people all around me who continue to experience marginalization. Hillel the Elder famously taught in *Pirkei Avot* (Ethics of the Sages), "If I am not for myself, who will be for me? Yet if I am only for myself, who am I?" Am I the best ally I can be to my Black and Indigenous friends and neighbours and congregants of colour? Am I the best ally I can be to my friends and neighbours and congregants and community members with disabilities? Am I using my voice and praying with my feet?

As we journey from Passover, the holiday of redemption, to Shavuot, the holiday of revelation, may I do all that I can to be a better ally.

Allyship as a Mitzvah: "You Must Raise Up With Them"

Rabbi Guy Austrian

Allyship is commonly understood as a choice to empathize with another and to act in support of their interests; a praiseworthy but ultimately optional act of generosity. Yet Judaism offers an alternative understanding of allyship as a *mitzvah*—a commandment, obligation, and spiritual imperative.

לֹא-תִרְאֶה אֶת-חֲמוֹר אָחִיךָ אוֹ שׁוֹרוֹ נֹפְלִים בַּדֶּרֶךְ, וְהִתְעַלַּמְתָּ
מֵהֶם; הָקֵם תָּקִים עִמּוֹ (דברים כב, ד)

> Do not see your fellow's donkey or ox fallen along the path, and ignore them; you must indeed raise up with [your fellow]. (Deuteronomy 22:4)

This mitzvah combines a negative injunction not to ignore, with a positive injunction to raise up, "*hakeim takim imo.*" What makes this a case of allyship is the last word *imo*, "with them (singular)." Raising up is not a one-sided act of charity in which an onlooker swoops in to save their fellow, but rather an act of solidarity in which the onlooker joins their fellow in a shared effort. The one who comes to assist does not direct the other in any way, but only supports them in their progress *baderech*, "along the path" that the other has chosen.

As with many other *mitzvot,* Jewish texts articulate values by considering the ethical and holy way to act in various scenarios. A parallel text describes a similar case with important differences:

כִּי-תִרְאֶה חֲמוֹר שֹׂנַאֲךָ רֹבֵץ תַּחַת מַשָּׂאוֹ, וְחָדַלְתָּ מֵעֲזֹב לוֹ, עָזֹב
תַּעֲזֹב עִמּוֹ. (שמות כג, ה)

> When you see the donkey of your enemy lying under its burden and would refrain from releasing it, you must indeed release it with them. (Exodus 23:5).

Here the onlooker is challenged to respond not merely to a fellow, but to an adversary. The animal has not yet fallen, but is actively struggling under its burden. The action required is to release the burden, but perhaps not to reload and raise up the animal. Regardless, this verse, like its counterpart, emphasizes the obligation to act *imo,* "with them." We might think that these mitzvot primarily aim to relieve the suffering of the animal, known as *tza'ar ba'alei chayim.* But for the ancient Rabbis, these scenarios are really about the relationship between two people—the animal's owner and the onlooker—and the cultivation in the onlooker of allyship.

The Rabbis get at this mindset by comparing scenarios:

אוהב לטעון ושונא לפרוק—מצוה לפרוק עם השונא, שלא
לשכור את לבו. (תוספתא, בבא מציעא ב, יא)

Between a friend who needs reloading, and an enemy who needs unburdening, the *mitzvah* is to unburden with one's enemy [first], so as not to reward one's heart. (Tosefta, Bava Metzia 2:11)

The enemy's animal needs help more urgently, yet the Tosefta teaches that we prioritize it not because of the animal's pain, but rather because we need to resist indulging our tendency to help our friends first.

A parallel text sharpens the Rabbis' motivation still further:

אוהב לפרוק ושונא לטעון—מצוה בשונא, כדי לכוף את יצרו. (תלמוד בבלי, בבא מציעא לב, ב)

Between a friend who needs unburdening, and an enemy who needs reloading, the mitzvah is to help one's enemy [first], so as to subjugate one's inclination. (Babylonian Talmud, Bava Metzia 32b)

Here, the *friend* is in the more urgent situation, and the enemy could wait to be helped. Yet even with our friend suffering more, still the *mitzvah* is to help the enemy first! And the reason why is stated forcefully: not merely that we avoid rewarding our inclination to do the easy thing, but rather to actively master that inclination and train ourselves to do the more difficult thing.

Allyship in these scenarios isn't easy. It isn't just about helping the people we like and building on those relationships. It's about extending ourselves to collaborate even with those we find difficult, even with those with whom we have tension, even with those who might not give us kudos and thanks before continuing on their path.

Allyship is also complicated. In the Mishnah (Bava Metzia 2:10), the Rabbis offer several additional lessons:

פרק וטען פרק וטען, אפילו ארבעה וחמשה פעמים—חייב,
שנאמר (שמות כג, ה) "עזב תעזב"

If one unloaded and reloaded, unloaded and reloaded, even four or five times, one is still obligated, as it is written, "You must indeed release" (Exodus 23:5).

Here the doubled form of the words *azov ta'azov* is understood to refer to repetition. Allyship isn't a one-time action. Like any spiritual discipline, it's a long-term commitment and an iterative practice (and one which we can get better at and understand more deeply with time). The Mishnah continues:

הלך וישב לו ואמר: הואיל ועליך מצוה, אם רצונך לפרוק,
פרוק—פטור, שנאמר "עמו". אם היה זקן או חולה—חייב

> If [the animal's owner] went and sat down and said: "Since this mitzvah is on you, if you want to unload, unload," then [the onlooker] is exempt, for it is said, "with them (*imo*)". [But] if [the animal's owner] was elderly or ill, then [the onlooker] is obligated.

Here we learn that allyship is not about taking orders or being taken for granted. Although the one who needs support knows the size and shape of the burden and how to handle it, and the would-be ally is obligated to help, still the Torah envisions a cooperative effort. At the same time, those who need support may be unable to accomplish certain tasks, in which case they may certainly indicate what needs doing by allies, who are obligated to take on those tasks, even by themselves.

Still more complexity is considered in other teachings in the same chapter of the Tosefta. For example, if it's Passover and the animal is loaded with *chametz,* leavened grain products forbidden on Passover, then the onlooker is not obligated to handle it (2:9). The same holds true if the animal is loaded with *yayin nesech*, wine used for idolatrous rituals (2:11). In other words, not every act of allyship is obligatory on every person at every time, especially if the action or the interpersonal relationship might be harmful to the would-be ally's own well-being.

What emerges from a brief study of these foundational texts is that allyship involves a dance of factors, situational, relational, and more, which challenges us to understand our obligation and to choose the right course of action in each scenario.

Like the people in the two verses of the Torah, we all are walking along a path, wrestling with our various burdens. The Torah wants us to learn to perceive when others are *nofelim baderech,*

132

stumbling along the way, and to pause along our own path in order to help others along theirs. The encounter is an opportunity to train our hearts to do the right thing, even the harder thing. And if that encounter is truly shared and collaborative, then we find that the effort to help another along their path actually becomes a part of our own.

"*Hakeim takim imo.* You will indeed raise up, together." Allyship is a mitzvah, and also a promise. When we lift up those around us, we too will be elevated. And we'll all be more likely to get where we're going.

An Ally in Waiting

Rabbi Hara E Person

Having privilege obligates us to be allies, to lend our support, voice, power, resources, and influence to help right an imbalance. Allyship is in part intuitive: we have and so we should share, we can and so we should do. And it is also an obligation about how we interact in the social justice landscape: where do we see injustice and what can we do to make things right? Allyship comes from both a place of want and a sense of obligation: I *want* to right an imbalance, and I am *obligated* to seek justice. True allyship involves a sense of ongoing moral obligation, not merely a wish to feel like a good person for an afternoon.

Not all opportunities for allyship live in the world we encounter when we open our front door and walk outside. Some forms of allyship, and arguably the most important, take place within our home, our families, around the table, and in our most intimate spaces. As our feminist foremothers taught, the personal is indeed political. Our family relationships potentially present a myriad of ways to ally. What is especially challenging though is that while some of these forms of allyship may be appreciated or even requested, others may not be as welcome.

One of the most familiar teachings from Torah is "honor your father and mother" (Exodus 20:12). The same sentiment, but phrased slightly differently, appears again later in the Torah:

"Revere your mother and father" (Lev 19:3). The Talmud explains that to *revere* a parent is to not usurp their place, not contradict their opinions, and not choose sides when the parent disagrees with someone, whereas to *honor* a parent is to provide food, clothing, and shelter, and care for their needs (BT Kiddushin 31b). Caring for a parent, therefore, involves attending to their behavioral, emotional, and physical needs, as well as potentially their medical, financial, and legal needs.

In the listing of commandments in Exodus, the requirement to honor one's parents is followed by, "that you may live long on the land that G-d is giving you" (Ex 20:12). This is the only mitzvah within that grouping that has an accompanying promise, as if this is the commandment that is so difficult that it needs an overt incentive, beyond simply obeying G-d. We need to be told to do so, because it can be difficult and not necessarily rewarding. Unlike caring for our children, which, while certainly challenging at times, we are supposedly biologically programmed to do, caring for our parents is not necessarily intuitive. As part of differentiating and becoming independent adults, many of us create some distance from our parents, even where there is an abundance of love and good will. And in some cases, there is even more distance created by hurt, different ways of seeing the world, or even trauma. As our parents age and need more from us, the question of how to engage and on what terms comes to the foreground. Taking care of our aging parents can be painful and heart-wrenching, something we might choose to avoid if we could.

The Torah teaches that one who insults his father or mother is to be put to death (Ex 21:17). That the Torah even needs to record this instruction might indicate that there are times when insulting one's parent is an instinctive reaction, or at least not a highly unusual occurrence. Moreover, we are not commanded to love our parents, but rather to honor and revere them. As the Talmud reminds us in differentiating between "revere" and "honor," this obligation is not merely emotional but actually practical. While love is lovely, we are obligated to care for our parents' needs and dignity regardless of our emotional attachment.   That is where allyship enters the equation.

I am at a time in my life where I believe it is necessary to be an ally to my aging mother. I have all the things that would make me a good ally: power, resources, technology know-how, compassion. I stand ready to offer help, both practical and emotional. I can pay bills, I can arrange appointments, I can check voicemails, I can make sure there is follow up where needed. I can offer friendship, companionship, books to read, meals to enjoy. I can clean up the apartment, I can clean out the fridge. I can interface with entities like the IRS and credit card companies. And yet here is a situation in which my attempts at allyship are thwarted at every turn. All offers are rejected. Pride and the desire for independence get in the way. And even so, the construction of competency is beginning to fray, pieces fall off, the center no longer holds.

I find comfort in the Talmudic teaching that the broken shards of the tablets were placed in the Ark of the Covenant along with the whole tablets. We are taught that these broken tablets, though far from perfect and not usable, were still to be considered sacred and were not to be treated with any less respect than the whole tablets. And this teaching goes on even more compassionately, comparing these broken fragments to an elder who has forgotten the wisdom they once possessed (Berachot 8b). My mother's mind may be unravelling, and she is surely no longer the capable, wise professor, author, mother, or grandmother she once was. Her decisions are poor and even put her in jeopardy, and her lapses in memory lead her down paths that are fraught and ill-advised. But even in this disintegrated state, she is still to be treated with dignity and honor, despite my frustration, feelings of helplessness, and even, at times, anger.

I want to help my mother because I love her, and also because our tradition obligates me to do so. Yet as much as I want to be her ally and honor her by taking on the responsibility of caring for her and her needs, the commandment to revere my mother means that I must wait until she is ready, or until she can no longer refuse. To revere her means, as the Talmud reminds me, not usurping her place as a decision-making or taking away her agency to determine her choices.

When we think of being a good ally, we often think of acting in a way that our ally wants or even requests. In this case, I am, for the moment, only a silent ally-in-waiting, ready to spring into action when circumstances will allow. Just because I believe she needs me as an ally doesn't mean, for the time being, that I get to make that decision. In the meantime, I care for the shards, making sure from the sidelines that they are housed comfortably within the ark. This, too, is a kind of justice on an intimate scale. And as I wait, I continue to learn how I can be a better ally. I survey the situation, I take in new information, I create partnerships, so that when the time comes, all the learning that I have done can be put to use.

Our Sameness & Otherness: Reaching for Allyship with G-d and with Humanity

Rabbi Shmuly Yanklowitz

When we see suffering, we should ideally feel emotions beyond pity and sympathy. We need to move towards empathy. We don't look down upon others who need help. Rather, we get to feel with them, lift each other up, and put ourselves in their position. This is what it means to be a friend. But there are two types of friendships: intimate-friend and ally-friend. An intimate-friend is someone we commit to in totality. An ally-friend is someone we may know less well, but nonetheless, we commit to their cause, identity, and security.

And even more extraordinarily, there is the enemy transformed into an ally-friend. We don't have total trust in them but we work toward solidarity with them. As the rabbis record:

> Who is the greatest of heroes? One who conquers one's own impulse (to evil), as it is said, "Better to be slow to anger than mighty; better to rule over one's own spirit than conquer a city" (Proverbs 16:32). And others say, '[Who is the greatest of heroes?] One who makes an enemy into a friend.' (Avot D'Rabbi Natan 23)

We do the hard work to turn enemies into allies not because it is fun or exciting, but rather because it is G-dly; it is *halakhta b'drachav* (*imitatio Dei*): the mitzvah of emulating G-d. As G-d stands as an ally with us, as partners in creation with us, so too, do we stand in partnership with others who differ from us. Our genders, sexual orientations, races, socio-economic statuses, cultures may be so different, but we see our human commonalities in our emotions and in our blood. And so, we reach beyond ourselves. To foster allyship between G-d and allyship with humans, the two merge together in the concept of *Tzelem Elokim*: the G-dliness found in every person. Indeed, we make a blessing ("Who revives the dead") when we haven't seen a friend for an extended period of time.

Allyship is a life and death matter. Consider this Talmudic passage about Honi, who was a kind of miracle worker famous for his ability to bring rain. After a well-known story about an encounter between Honi and old man planting a carob tree, which takes about seventy years to bear fruit, Honi asks:

> "Why do you plant it? You won't be around in seventy years." The man responds: "When I came into the world, I found carob trees planted by my ancestors. I plant these for my descendants."

Honi falls asleep, and sleeps for seventy years. When he wakes up, no one recognizes him. He feels isolated and invisible. His overwhelming loneliness leads him to pray for death, and he dies. Raba comments: "Hence the saying: either friendship or death" (Babylonian Talmud, Ta'anit 23A).

And this is why Rabbi Yehoshua ben Perachiah teaches: "Provide yourself a teacher, acquire for yourself a friend, and judge every person favorably (Pirkei Avot 1:6)." In a complementary passage, the rabbis explain:

> "'Acquire for yourself a friend.' How so? This teaches that a person should get a companion to eat with, drink with, study with, sleep with, and reveal secrets, the secrets of the Torah and the secrets of worldly things (Avot d'Rabbi Natan 8:3)."

Maimonides, not known to have free time for a social life, nonetheless teaches that:

> Friends are something that is necessary for a person throughout life... In a state of health and happiness, a person takes pleasure in a friend's familiar relationship; in adversity, the person has recourse to them; and in old age when the body is grown weak, the person seeks their help.

Maimonides elucidates that "a person requires friends all their lifetime" (*The Guide for the Perplexed*, 3:49). Furthermore, Maimonides analyzes the Mishna to create three levels of friendship. The lowest level is a friendship based on mutual benefit (*chaver l'davar*) such as the relationship between business associates. Rambam then divides the next level in two: friendship based on pleasure, and friendship based on security; both comprise friendship based on a sense of equilibrium, but the latter sub-level is higher. Friendship based on security is such that each person finds in the other someone whom he can trust; someone with whom he can let down his defenses, and share all profound matters and innermost thoughts, good and bad, without fear. The highest level of friendship is *chaver l'de'ah*, a friendship of a lofty character: both friends aspire to the point where each partner feels responsible for helping the other to grow in self-understanding.

Betty Friedan, the late thinker on feminism and gender, wrote in *The Fountain of Age:*

> More and more, psychologists have found that for older persons, loneliness is not necessarily linked to the death of a spouse or to how infrequently they see their children or grandchildren, but to the absence of personal relationships with peers, friends of their own age or any age who share their interests and with whom they sustain their roots of shared experience.

In contrast to his later acolyte Maimonides, Aristotle's three kinds of friendship (pleasure, utility, and virtue) often tend to understand friendships in a descending order of convenience (*Nicomachean Ethics, Book VIII*). Spiritual leadership helps address these deficiencies. Indeed, being an ally is not about playing a sport together (pleasure), or running errands for one another (utility), but about virtue and the ability to cultivate the best traits within ourselves in partnership with another human being. The moral philosopher Alasdair MacIntyre, who frequently references Aristotle and other classical philosophers, explains: "In achieving accountability we will have learned not only how to speak to, but also how to speak for the other. We will, in the home or in the workplace or in other shared activity, have become—in one sense of that word—friends."

The process of allyship means ensuring others don't feel or stand alone. We don't have to understand everything they know or feel everything they feel. But we need to see the other and hear the other. The Talmud teaches that in religious learning and growth, a friend is even more important than a teacher: "I have learned much from my teachers, but from my friends more than my teachers" (Babylonian Talmud, Ta'anit 7a). A friend of virtue is more connected to our intimate life pursuits more than any teacher can be. Thus, the rabbis teach that "one is not even to part from one's friend without exchanging words of Torah" (Babylonian Talmud, Berakhot 31a). A friend, on the highest level, is primarily a learning partner and a partner in life.

We don't stand as allies for a moment but commit to an ongoing evolving journey together of learning and discovery.

Based on his reading of the Book of Job, Rabbi Joseph Soloveitchik explains that there is a vital spiritual purpose to friendships: "Job certainly did not grasp the meaning of friendship. At this phase, even communal and social relations served the purpose of utility and safety. Real friendship is possible only when man rises to the height of an open existence, in which he is capable of prayer and communication. In such living, the personality fulfills itself" (Out of the Whirlwind, 154). It is not until Job realizes the importance of opening himself spiritually to others that he truly comes to understand the value of friendship: "And the Lord returned the fortunes of Job, when he prayed for his friends; and the Lord gave Job twice as much as he had before" (Job 42:10).

But the basis of all this holy work is love. "Any love that is dependent upon a specific cause, when the cause is gone, the love is gone; but if it does not depend on a specific cause, it will never cease" (Pirkei Avot 5:16).

We live in an era where rancor and division tear our society asunder. There are pernicious elements in our society that would gain from keeping people at each other's throats. But we can resist. And when we resist, we affirm that friendship, love, and peace are the foundations of society that we want to make manifest in the world today. Through the crucial building block of true, earnest, and empathetic allyship, may we learn together, fight for each other together, and keep the flames of love alive for a brighter tomorrow.

To Believe That Another's Truth is True: Humility and Empathy at the Core of Allyship

Rabbi Stephanie Kolin

I was so incredibly nervous. My hands were shaking, I was cold and then hot and then both at the same time. I was home from my sophomore year of college, and I was going to tell someone very dear to me that I had fallen in love. With a woman. I hadn't told anyone yet and I was really sweating this. To be honest, I wasn't even sure how I was going to get the words out of my mouth. I calmed myself with the knowledge that this person I was going to tell was gay and surely, *surely*, they were going to be warm and happy for me and full of love. And, in fact, they were! I was so lucky. I knew it then and I know it now.

And it is also true that that same conversation ended terribly. I told them that I didn't really identify as any particular category, but if I had to put a name to it, I was bisexual. They told me that there is no such thing. I looked up from anxiously wringing my hands with confusion. I thought maybe I had misunderstood. I asked what they meant, and they said, "eventually you choose," as if that were enough to explain what felt like such a betrayal in the moment. Eventually, they continued, you get married to someone, so you are whatever you end up being. I said nothing. I wasn't up for the fight and I never brought it up again.

I knew a truth about myself and whether someone else would dismiss it as a fiction, an impossibility, or a naivete, did not change who I was nor who I would be when and if I married. But wow did that hurt. My young gaslit heart felt injured enough that I remember this conversation more than twenty years later. For a few fleeting moments, I had an ally. And then they were gone.

Over time, I realized what had happened that day. They simply did not have the same lived experience as I did, and they were not willing to believe that what I was describing was true. And I think at the center of this encounter is where I learned something important about what it means to be an ally.

In Pirkei Avot, we learn וְאַל תָּדִין אֶת חֲבֵרְךָ עַד שֶׁתַּגִּיעַ לִמְקוֹמוֹ, do not judge your friend until you have arrived to his place. This probably sounds like an early version of "Don't judge a man until you've walked a mile in his shoes," which is a later version of a teaching of the Cherokee Nation. This is ancient wisdom. It reminds us that we can't possibly judge the veracity of another person's experience, for we cannot possibly understand it until we ourselves have lived it.

The S'fat Emet expands this idea, teaching that it is impossible for anyone to *ever* reach the place of their fellow, for not all people's mindsets are the same. We might add that not all people's skin color, gender, sexuality, ability, access to resources, and so on, are the same. Therefore, he says, do not judge your fellow at all.

What does this mean? What can we draw from this caution as we seek to better understand what it means to be a good ally? That a good first step toward allyship is to find the humility to say that we can't intimately know what someone else's lived experience might be, but that we choose to trust that they themselves do. Imagine the transformational partnerships and solidarity that we could build if we embrace the words of the S'fat Emet and withhold our judgment about whether another person's truth is, in fact true.

This work is not easy. Allyship is not easy. We know we want it in theory, but we seem to be built to give primacy to our own truths and experiences. Of course we do! We swim in the waters of our own lives every second of the day. But this world is profoundly broken, and we need one another to wade through the muck of it. To endure the waves of suffering together and to be powerful enough to make this world more just and compassionate. We are all in need of allies, partners, co-conspirators in the work of justice.

It begins by seeing each other, hearing each other, and believing each other. White people, believing Black people when they speak about the daily and exhausting microaggressions they face. Cisgendered people believing the heart of one who says they are not the gender they were assigned at birth. Believing asylum seekers who trust us with the terror they fled. Believing people who are differently abled who describe living in a world that dismisses their worth. It all begins with agreeing that we could not possibly know another person's journey for we haven't journeyed it in their body.

Preparing ourselves to be allies in this way is a lot harder than it sounds, I think, but without allies, we find ourselves in a sharp-edged world that is "every man for himself," yearning for a world that is "all hands on deck." Over and over, so many find it worth the hard parts.

But if I can't know what it's like to live another's life, how can I understand what I need to do? Jewish tradition also teaches us that we have the power to understand each other by tapping into our own vulnerabilities and pain. In Exodus, we are told, "Do not oppress the stranger, for you know the soul of the stranger, having been strangers in the land of Egypt." This text gives us access to our empathy. We have been hurt, we know what hurt is like. We have felt alone, we know what loneliness is. It won't be the same experience, but it will carry the scent of understanding and it can draw our hearts to open in love. From the depths of that empathy, we have the power to be extraordinary allies across so many lines of difference.

If we want to be allies to those who face great injustice, if we want to have allies to confront the injustice we face, I offer four way-too-simple steps. First, believe a person who describes who and what they are. Second, listen with compassionate curiosity to learn more through their eyes. Third, ask how you can be helpful and what they need in your partnership. And fourth, lead. If you have a platform, use it. If you have a microphone, speak clearly into it. And when the opportunity comes along, hand it to someone whose voice is most often not heard.

I recently gave a sermon about gender and Jewish tradition, noting the wide spectrum of gender and sex in our classical texts. After the service, someone shared for the first time with those schmoozing on the Zoom that they are gender non-conforming, and that they were grateful to feel so seen. I am a cisgendered woman, but it is my responsibility to affirm that other experiences of gender are also true. As an ally with a microphone, I try to use it in ways that help make our world more whole. I also make plenty of mistakes. We all do and will, but the real loss would be in finding ourselves alone in a world so in need of community. I am grateful for the day I was told that what I am doesn't exist, so that I could learn how to be a better ally today. I am still learning.

Smashing Idols, Building Allies

Rabbi Michael Adam Latz

My husband and I have tried to teach our kids to be polite, to always say "please" and "thank you." In fact, a rule in our household is, "You do not need to like everyone, but you must be kind." It's a good rule to live by.

I'm struck as I read Lech Lecha and the story of Avram and Sarai's journey from their homeland to set forth on their journey from G-d. The Midrash teaches that the impetus for Avram's departure is the brutal smashing of his father's idols: what his father believed to be G-ds. It's hardly a kind or a polite act. How is it possible that the founder of our people got his start in the world trashing other people's religious faith? Conversely, had he not rejected the faith of his father, would he have charted a new course and started our people?

We look to another religious journey to seek clarity, the story of our collective liberation from Egypt. Moshe tried going before Pharaoh and politely asking for Pharaoh to liberate the Israelite people. As we know, Pharaoh declined. In turn, G-d sent plague after plague to Pharaoh.

Those ten plagues were as much to challenge the Egyptians and Pharaoh as they were to show the Israelites that we had the power of endurance; the plagues helped the Israelites slaves build the requisite faith and the spiritual muscles to resist tyranny.

Those 10 plagues were the original politics of disruption; humanity's boldest wakeup call:

You beat these slaves? We're gonna ruin your water!

You overwork these people? We're gonna wreck your crops!

You won't pay them? We're gonna block your roads!

You won't free them? We're gonna turn off the lights!

You deny people their basic human dignity? We're coming!

After ten plagues, Pharaoh's hardened heart finally shattered and our people marched to freedom.

Why?

Because enslaving people, discriminating against people, denying people our innate dignity is such a profound theological affront to G-d that business as usual just isn't possible. We must never forget where we've come from and who we are: we were slaves in the land of Egypt, you and I; those are the words we recite every Passover seder.

Human dignity is our ultimate theological concern. And when that means interrupting business as usual to break the chains of bondage, then it is both our religious inheritance and our moral obligation to rise up against the tyranny that prevents all people from being fully human.

I do *not* advocate violence. I *do* support

creating discomfort in pursuit of justice and human dignity.

Devontae Torriente, an African American leader, explains, "It's time for us to do away with the idea that we must be respectful or courteous to be entitled to our rights. Politeness isn't a requirement when we are confronting anyone who uses their political and social power to further disenfranchise us. We are now charged with ushering in a new era of normalized discomfort in which people in positions of power that in this fight for our humanity, we will not concede the raw power of our indignation. In this age of entitlement by those with problematic or seemingly unpopular views, remember this: I don't owe you my tolerance, especially not when my life is at stake."[10]

As DeRay Mckesson offers pointedly, "If your love for me requires that I hide parts of who I am, then you don't love me. Love is never a request for silence."[11]

As we journey this spring from Egypt to Sinai, from Pesach to Shavuot, we are offered an invitation: An invitation to hold the story of Abraham smashing the idols and the plagues

---

10 Torriente, D. (2017). "I Don't Owe You My Tolerance: How 'Civil Discourse' Functions to Uphold Systems of Oppression." *The Blackprint.* (June 17).
11 Mckesson, D. [@deray]. (2015/5/3). If your love for me requires that I hide parts of who I am, then you don't love me. Love is never a request for silence. [TWEET] Twitter. https://twitter.com/deray/status/595085132228362241?s=20

when we left Egypt. An invitation to behold the powerful words of Devontae Torriente and DeRay Mckesson. An invitation to embrace the discontent and discomfort that comes from important, meaningful change and transformation. An invitation to be allies in the project of authentic social healing, to seek true justice, even when it creates discomfort, especially when it demands our full integrity.

I pray with all my being that we can emerge from this moment of global tumult ever more compassionate, just, and whole: even when it means we must be a little less polite.

We Rise to Speak

Rabbi Avi Strausberg

When their father Tzelafchad dies, his daughters Mahlah, Noah, Hoglah, Milkah, and Tirzah find themselves without claim to their own land. They lack the rights of the male inheritor and, in the patriarchal world of the Torah, their father's land would pass to the nearest male relative. In the Torah (Numbers 27:1), we read:

וַתִּקְרַבְנָה בְּנוֹת צְלׇפְחָד בֶּן־חֵפֶר בֶּן־גִּלְעָד בֶּן־מָכִיר בֶּן־מְנַשֶּׁה לְמִשְׁפְּחֹת מְנַשֶּׁה בֶן־יוֹסֵף וְאֵלֶּה שְׁמוֹת בְּנֹתָיו מַחְלָה נֹעָה וְחׇגְלָה וּמִלְכָּה וְתִרְצָה׃

> The daughters of Tzelafchad, of Manassite family, son of Hepher son of Gilead son of Machir son of Manasseh son of Joseph, drew near. The names of the daughters were Mahlah, Noah, Hoglah, Milkah, and Tirzah.

In a modern midrash written by Rivka Lubitz, she asks why the daughters were first identified as the daughters of Tzelafchad and, only after they drew near, identified as individuals each with their own name? She answers by making a linguistic connection to the name Tzelafchad and the Hebrew words for fear and shadow. As long as their father Tzelafchad lived, they lived *b'tzel v'fachad*, in the shade of their father, afraid to raise their heads.

155

It was only after their father's death that the daughters drew near to one another, and in doing so, they drew strength from each other. Lubitz rereads the opening of the story in which *vatikravna* is usually translated as "the daughters drew near" to Moses in order to plead their case instead to mean "first they drew near to each other." Only then were they emboldened to raise their heads and demand justice within the patriarchal system in which they were bound. On this Midrash, Rabbi Jessica Kate Meyer writes, "before they approached the male authority, they approached each other. They gave each other permission and courage... Only when they approached each other, listened to each other, took counsel with each other, could they access a font of courage, to step out of that shadow, and to approach, as a collective, the halls of power and do what no one had ever done before."

In other words, the daughters act as each other's allies. On their own, they lived in the shadow and fear of the patriarchy, unable to demand justice. Together, they supported each other, they strengthened each other, and amplified each other's voices so that their case could be heard and brought before Moses and G-d. In the daily liturgy of the morning prayer service, in the opening blessings before the Shma, our liturgy imagines a choir of angels standing together, joining in voice and song to praise G-d. We assert that each and every angel is worthy and holy of praising G-d. We pray:

כֻּלָּם עוֹמְדִים בְּרוּם עוֹלָם וּמַשְׁמִיעִים בְּיִרְאָה יַחַד בְּקוֹל דִּבְרֵי אֱלֹהִים חַיִּים וּמֶלֶךְ עוֹלָם. כֻּלָּם אֲהוּבִים. כֻּלָּם בְּרוּרִים. כֻּלָּם גִּבּוֹרִים. וְכֻלָּם עוֹשִׂים בְּאֵימָה וּבְיִרְאָה רְצוֹן קוֹנָם. וְכֻלָּם פּוֹתְחִים אֶת־פִּיהֶם בִּקְדֻשָּׁה וּבְטָהֳרָה. בְּשִׁירָה וּבְזִמְרָה. וּמְבָרְכִים וּמְשַׁבְּחִים וּמְפָאֲרִים וּמַעֲרִיצִים וּמַקְדִּישִׁים וּמַמְלִיכִים אֶת שֵׁם הָאֵל הַמֶּלֶךְ...

All stand at the height of the Universe, and proclaim with reverence, in unison aloud the words of the living G-d, King of the Universe. All of them are beloved, all of them are pure, all of them are mighty and all of them perform with awe and reverence the will of their Possessor. And they all open their mouths in holiness and purity, with song and music, and they bless, and praise, and glorify, and revere, and sanctify, and proclaim the sovereignty of the Name of the Almighty...

Each and every angel is holy and worthy of G-d's presence; each and every angel's voice is necessary in the praise of G-d. Then, we pray:

וְכֻלָּם מְקַבְּלִים עֲלֵיהֶם עֹל מַלְכוּת שָׁמַיִם זֶה מִזֶּה. וְנוֹתְנִים רְשׁוּת זֶה לָזֶה לְהַקְדִּישׁ לְיוֹצְרָם בְּנַחַת רוּחַ...

And they all take upon themselves the yoke of Divine sovereignty one from the other, and give permission to one another to sanctify their Creator in a spirit of serenity with clear speech and pleasantness...

The angels are each other's allies in prayer. First, they recognize that each and every angel is holy and worthy in the service of G-d. Then, they give permission to one another to open their mouths in prayer. They give permission to each other to serve G-d in the fullness of their selves, as beings worthy of Divine love.

What if we were to give permission to each other to open our mouths in prayer? What if we were to give permission to each other to serve G-d in the fullness of our humanity, each of us beings worthy of Divine love? What if, like Mahlah, Noah, Heglah, Milkah, and Tirzah, we came together to demand justice, finding strength and support in each other to come out from the shadows and ask for what we deserve?

In Marge Piercy's poem, "Amidah: On Our Feet We Speak To You," she begins,

We rise to speak
A web of bodies aligned like notes of music...
Yet you have taught us to push against the walls,
To reach out and pull each other along,
To strive to find the way through
If there is no way around, to go on.

Echoing the language of the *Kedushah* of the *Amidah* in which the angels call out to G-d in praise, she continues:

We will try to be holy,

We will try to repair the world given us to hand on.

Precious is this treasure of words and knowledge and deeds that moves inside us,

Holy is the hand that works for peace and for justice,

Holy is the mouth that speaks for goodness

Holy is the foot that walks toward mercy.

Let us lift each other on our shoulders and carry each other along.

Let holiness move in us.

Let us pay attention to its small voice,

Let us see the light in others and honor that light.

Like angels who give permission to each other to praise G-d, we too join together, a web of bodies to reach out and pull each other along. Like the angels, each one holy and worthy of G-d's Divine love, we assert that we too will try to be holy, we too will try to work for justice. When we draw near to each other in allyship, we can lift each other up, we can carry each other along, and only then can we come out from the shadows of fear. As we give each other permission to speak, as we affirm each other's holiness and amplify each other's voices, may we create a world of light, in which the light of every human being is seen and honored.

Being G-d's Allies

Rabbi Avram Mlotek

An ally is to be a teammate, to be a part of a larger whole. "Do not extricate yourself from the community," the rabbis counsel. "All of Israel is intertwined," we learn. And so, for those who have been outcast in our community because of their sex, sexuality, gender, or whatever other prejudice imposed, it is incumbent upon the larger Jewish community to serve as allies for those suffering: to stand with them and by them, not for their sakes, but for ours.

Thousands of years ago, the prophet Micah summed up the Jewish charge: "Do justice, love kindness, walk humbly with your G-d." And yet, somehow, someway, we Jews, as diverse and splintered as we are, still scratch our heads and pontificate, wondering if justice and kindness *really* ought to extend to this marginalized group or that oppressed population. What *kind* of justice is the Torah talking about? What does it really *mean* to love kindness? *How* might one walk humbly?

The Psalmist writes that the earth is G-d's. This has led the rabbis to understand that we, humanity, are merely tenants here. People made of flesh and blood have an expiration date, coming from dust and returning to dust. "Who is wise?" ask the rabbis in Ethics of our Parents, "one who learns from all." The mandate becomes clearer: uphold the *tzelem elokim*, the spark of G-dliness, that is endowed in each and every human being we encounter. Walk the world knowing that whoever you may meet reflects G-d in some way and know that your time here is limited.

If we strive to walk in the world this way then we are not as preoccupied with the mental mathematics of who "deserves"our kindness or what "form" of justice "ought" to be administered. Instead, we become *ovdei haShem*, servants of G-d, striving to perfect the world. The Talmud in Beitzah 32b states emphatically: "Anyone who exhibits loving compassion is considered a descendant of Abraham our father, and any who are not lovingly compassionate - it is known that they are not descendants of Abraham our father." Forget who your mother is, what synagogue you go to, what conversion you might have. For the rabbis in this Gemara your behavior towards your fellow is what defines your lineage, your Jewishness.

Walking with G-d, as the prophet Micah prescribed, implies we are intended to be on G-d's side, G-d's allies. For me, serving an ally, means walking humbly with G-d. It is to act with compassion towards all, even and especially when I may not understand my fellow.

The Talmud teaches that it is impossible to disassociate how you engage with other people with how G-d views you; the two are intrinsically linked. (See Shabbat 151b). In fact, according to the Hasidic masters, it is us who are called directly to be allies for G-d. The Torah in Leviticus describes G-d stating to the people: "For you are strangers and residents with me." Rabbi Moshe Chaim Ephraim of Sudilkov, the Baal Shem Tov's grandson, in his work Degel Machaneh Ephraim, explains that this means: "G-d is like a stranger in this world, having no one on whom to rest the Divine presence." It is then incumbent upon us to create a dwelling place for G-d in this lower world of ours. We do so by emulating G-d's loving kindness. Once we become G-d's allies, we can become allies to G-d's children: humanity.

Moses calls out in Exodus, "Who is for Hashem? Come with me." The charge to love the *ger*, the other and not to oppress the *ger*, the stranger is the most repeated charge in the Torah. If this is not a call to allyship, what is?

Every Friday night we recite kiddush, the sanctification over the day of rest and wine. We bear witness to G-d's creation and remember the Exodus from Mitzrayim, the ancient land of Egypt. To witness is to say that I saw and took part in that sacred event. I was there. History is still unfolding and if we are to move from being bystanders to witnesses, we must become allies to those who need our help. Not because they need our help but because it is the Jew's moral responsibility to do so.

Ancestors as Allies: Honoring the Ones Who Came Before

Rav Kohenet Taya Mâ Shere

"Tell us about your ancestors."

This is the invitation that opens each episode of my Jewish Ancestral Healing podcast, in which I have the pleasure of speaking with spiritual leaders, artists, activists and visionaries about how they connect with their ancestors. While these sacred conversations happen with my dearest friends and collaborators, I've discovered that I rarely know anything specific about their ancestors until the podcast conversations begin. How is it that who and where they are from hasn't come up until now? How can we be strong allies, supporting each other to shine in our unique identities, if we don't know from whom each other comes?

Each of Us Has a Name[12]

In 2017, just after the period when Water Protectors convened in ceremonial action at Standing Rock Reservation to stop the drilling of the Dakota Access Pipeline, we had the great honor of welcoming award-winning filmmaker and Indigenous rights activist Fidel Moreno to a training retreat for Kohenet Hebrew Priestess

---

12 Drawn from the poem "Each of Us Has a Name" by the Israeli poet Zelda (Schneurson).

163

Institute,[13] which I co-founded. As Fidel opened his first session, a water ceremony and teaching, he spent the first forty-some minutes introducing himself by sharing his Huichol, Chichimeca and Mexican-American ancestry, and, in particular, naming the women, mother, aunts, grandmothers, who he came from.

I remember feeling antsy as Fidel shared name after name, story after story, wondering when he would get to the teaching, until I realized that this itself *was* the teaching. We couldn't receive his transmission until he had honored those who had shaped him, until we had received a context for his presence. Fidel's way of introduction, situating himself in the names and the stories of his people, is not so different from Jewish ways.

In Jewish tradition, our names often situate us in our lineages. In Ashkenazi tradition, many are named after beloved dead, and in Sephardi and Mizrahi tradition, many are named for living relatives. Throughout our lives we are named as *bat*, daughter of, *ben*, son of, or the non-binary *m'beit*, from the house of, reciting a litany of the names of our parents and their parents, chronicling the ones who have come before us. Our names are spoken this way when we are named at birth or conversion, when we are called

13 For more about Kohenet Hebrew Priestess Institute, devoted to reclaiming and innovating embodied, earth-based models of feminist Jewish spiritual leadership, see kohenet.com or *The Hebrew Priestess: Ancient and New Visions of Jewish Women's Spiritual Leadership* (Ben Yehuda Press, 2016) by Jill Hammer & Taya Shere.

to the Torah, when healing prayers are said on our behalf, and in the recitation of funerary prayer. And we tell the stories of our spiritual ancestors, the *avot v' imahot*, again and again, in Torah and Tanakh, during seders, and in everyday prayer services. Who we come from both intricately shapes and deeply drives our unique identities and our particular expressions of Judaism.

Rebuilding Relationship With Our Ancestors

While we root in the names of recent ones, and anchor our sacred cosmology around stories of ancient ones, there often exists an immense gap between the ancient matriarchs and patriarchs, and our most recent beloved dead. So much has been remembered, and so much has been obscured or erased in the years between.

Each of my grandmothers were powerhouse women, had immense gifts, and were deeply loving and highly resilient. They each experienced extreme trauma at pivotal moments in their lives. Beginning in my teens and continuing well into adulthood, I felt stuck in patterns connected to their highly specific traumas.

I attempted to transform the patterns through therapy, somatics and energetic healing. I tried to work the patterns directly with my grandmas: one who died when I was a child and the other for whom, as an adult, I offered extensive care until death. My attempts to heal through my deceased grandmas, through ritual and soul conversations, were to no avail.

It was inside of this wrestling and prayer that I encountered the modality of Ancestral Lineage Healing, which I now teach with an explicitly Jewish lens. This work asks us to approach healing ancestral trauma by rooting in positive resources in our ancestral lines.

I, like so many Jews, had huge gaps of knowledge about my lineage due to forced and chosen diaspora. Longstanding systemic oppressions, along with recent genocide, have led to forgetting and erasure: of stories, of traditions, of knowing the names and places of my people. This narrative of collective Jewish PTSD includes distinct expressions of intergenerational trauma for Jews of Sephardi, Mizrahi, and Asheknazi descent, and Jews of Color.

I longed to connect with long-ago ancestors of my blood lineages who were benevolent and loving, who wanted to be a source of blessing in my life and healing in my lines. When I dropped into a meditative state and sought my ancient ancestors, welcomed them, holding boundaries with the troubled dead and asking for the presence of loving and wise ancestral support, I was astonished by what came. Through meditative journeys, I encountered ancestral guides who are celebrating me, holding me, inspiring me: ancient ones who bless me, who are able to hold a cocoon of prayer to contain any lineal energy of fragment, trouble or distress, who are able to heal down through the line, generation by generation, that the troubled dead can become less troubled, and make their way fully home.

These ancient ones didn't only exist in the past. I felt them palpably as energetically present right now. I felt them as allies and support at my back.

What if the stories, teachings and traditions that have been erased, lost or forgotten are not fully gone?

What if, while we may not know their names, we can still connect with support and blessing of our loving and wise ancestors?

This is for some, a very big *"What If"*. For others, it is a *"Not Possible"*, or it is a *"Too Painful to Even Touch"*. For me, this has become not a *"What If"* but a *"Yes Please!"*

Ancestors Beyond Bloodlines

While ancestors of blood or family lineage are vitally important, we also come from ancient ancestry far beyond human: we are the stuff of stars, of minerals, of plants, of creatures from land and sea. We can honor ancestors of the more-than-human world[14] as our kin, understanding our place in the web of life, and showing up in allyship with the waters, soil, animal and plant life.

It is important, too, to acknowledge ancestors of place, and to recognize that wherever you are

---

14 The 'more-than-human world' is a phrase coined by Jewish ecologist and philospher David Abram in his book *The Spell of the Sensuous* (1996).

in this very moment, you work, play and live on land that was inhabited, loved and tended by earlier peoples. Honor the First Peoples of the places where you are, whose bodies have become the land, whose bones and blood are in the soil, whose homes are where you are blessed to be. Know their names and say them aloud at the beginning of ceremonies. Learn their traditions and histories. Show up in allyship with living ones of those communities and be in reciprocity and reparation. Pay a land tax honoring Indigenous land rights and sovereignty.[15]

Acknowledge, too, ancestors of movement and identity. Consider ways your work for justice has been inspired and made possible by the immense courage and devotion of the many in the movements before you. You might call on lineages of queer ancestors or transcestors as a source of inspiration and belonging. Appreciate, as well, ancestors of craft or vocation. Perhaps you are a birth worker, calling on the ancient midwives Shifra and Puah or the more recently ancestored Maude E. Callen[16] for their blessings, guidance and support when attending a birth. Perhaps you are a weaver, and feel yourself woven into the

---

15 Find additional resources for Jewish solidarity with Indigenous sovereignty through the work of Jews on Ohlone Land www.jewsonohloneland.com.
16 Maude E. Callen was a Black American nurse-midwife in the South Carolina Lowcountry for over 60 years. For more info:
https://scafricanamerican.com/honorees/maude-e-callen/.

tapestry of *orgot*, the weavers in the great temple, each time you sit at your loom. Or you call on these weaver ancestors when braiding a curriculum for a class that you teach.

An Invitation: Embracing Ancestors as Allies

Ancestors may be our allies whether we know it or not. It is entirely possible (dare I say likely) that you are amidst the loving support of your benevolent ancestors in this very moment. And, just like any relationship, devoting time, care, attention, showing-upness and reciprocity can deepens and enhance the strength of the connection we feel to our ancestors.

How might you welcome and lean into the support and allyship of your benevolent ancestors? Talk to your ancestors aloud, or invite connection with them through dreams. Cook family recipes, or ancestral foods from the regions your people are from. Place a stone beneath a neighborhood tree and visit it on your regular walks. Attune to your ancestors as you light Shabbat candles, knead challah dough, or braid your hair. Ask your ancestors the questions that are most alive on your heart.

May you always feel the support of your loving and wise ancestors at your back.

Allyship and the Omer

Rabbi Ayelet S. Cohen

Like the *omer*, the time between the early spring harvest of Pesach and the summer harvest of Shavuot, being an ally is about witnessing, exercising patience, and constancy.

Allyship starts with listening. It starts with being present with your beloved fellow.

The *omer* is a time of active watching and listening, of paying attention to subtle changes in the earth and the sky. Perhaps you helped plant the seeds, or you have helped prune and weed and water. But mostly it's out of our hands. The *omer* is about patience.

שִׁבְעָ֥ה שָׁבֻעֹ֖ת תִּסְפָּר־לָ֑ךְ מֵהָחֵ֤ל חֶרְמֵשׁ֙ בַּקָּמָ֔ה תָּחֵ֣ל לִסְפֹּ֔ר שִׁבְעָ֖ה שָׁבֻעֽוֹת:

> Seven weeks shall you count for yourself; from the beginning of the sickle in the standing corn shall you begin to count seven weeks (Deuteronomy 16:9).

The farmers had done everything within their power to prepare and tend the land. The next portion of the growing season beyond their control. They felt their vulnerability to the elements keenly.

The rabbis understood the time of the *omer* to be part of the ongoing annual cycle of divine judgement and blessings. Judgement, they believed, did not end on Yom Kippur; rather every day of the year provided opportunities for the Divine to witness our deeds and bestow blessing. Each day gave us the opportunity to pray for healing; the state of the crops in the fields provided a window into whether G-d was inclined to bestow favor in the form of a successful harvest.

I don't believe that Divine presence or judgement manifests in the form of adequate sun and rain. Yet I relate on a very deep level to the sense of vulnerability, and to knowing that a positive outcome is most often not within our control. It is within our power to make things worse, through neglect or malpractice; it is within our power to do all that we can to create the conditions for progress and success. Beyond that we must wait, and listen, and watch. And pray.

תַּנְיָא אָמַר רַבִּי יְהוּדָה מִשׁוּם רַבִּי עֲקִיבָא מִפְּנֵי מָה אָמְרָה תּוֹרָה הָבִיאוּ עוֹמֶר בַּפֶּסַח מִפְּנֵי שֶׁהַפֶּסַח זְמַן תְּבוּאָה הוּא אָמַר הַקָּדוֹשׁ בָּרוּךְ הוּא הָבִיאוּ לְפָנַי עוֹמֶר בַּפֶּסַח כְּדֵי שֶׁתִּתְבָּרֵךְ לָכֶם תְּבוּאָה שֶׁבַּשָּׂדוֹת וּמִפְּנֵי מָה אָמְרָה תּוֹרָה הָבִיאוּ שְׁתֵּי הַלֶּחֶם בָּעֲצֶרֶת מִפְּנֵי שֶׁעֲצֶרֶת זְמַן פֵּירוֹת הָאִילָן הוּא אָמַר הַקָּדוֹשׁ בָּרוּךְ הוּא הָבִיאוּ לְפָנַי שְׁתֵּי הַלֶּחֶם בַּעֲצֶרֶת כְּדֵי שֶׁיִּתְבָּרְכוּ לָכֶם פֵּירוֹת הָאִילָן

It is taught in a *baraita* that Rabbi Yehuda said in the name of Rabbi Akiva: "For what reason did the Torah say: Bring the *omer* offering on the second day of Passover? It is because Passover is the time of grain, the beginning of the grain harvest season, and therefore the Holy Blessed One said: Bring the *omer* offering before Me on Passover so that

171

the grain in the fields will be blessed for you."
And for what reason did the Torah say: "Bring
the offering of the two loaves from the new
wheat on *Shavuot*? It is because *Shavuot* is the
time of the fruits that grow on a tree, when it
begins to ripen, and therefore the Holy
Blessed One said: Bring the offering of the two
loaves before Me on *Shavuot* so that the fruits
that grow on a tree will be blessed for you"
(Rosh Hashanah 16:a).

The vulnerability and the lack of control of
omer time can be hard to tolerate, especially for
allies who are used to being able to accomplish
what we want to do. Those of us who frequently
dwell in the majority may be used to being heard
when we speak and being effective when we act.
The *omer* can remind us that change takes time. It
can remind us that being an ally is not about me.
It's about being useful in this moment. What does
my beloved fellow need today? They are the
expert in their experience and thus they are my
guide. So we ask ourselves as allies, what skills or
platform or credibility or relationships do I have,
in this moment, that I can channel in service of
what my loved one needs.

On Pesach the liturgy in the daily Amida prayer
changes from "*morid hageshem*" to "*morid hatal.*"
We cease our daily prayer for rain, and in the
Sephardic and Land of Israel tradition begin a
daily prayer for dew. At this point in the harvest,
we need more subtle intervention. But often
when the change needed is more subtle, more

nuanced, less dramatic, that's when the allies fall away, thinking that they have done the job. Thinking that the work is done.

Being an ally isn't about showing up for the big moments, although sometimes it's that too. It's not about swooping in when there is a crisis. It's about every day. Think of the harvest. If you showed up on planting day and harvest day, it would feel great, and the extra help would likely be needed. If you also showed up when there was a hailstorm, that would be helpful, and you would do some good. But what about the other days? Are you there to water and prune? And on most days, the days you're not there? Are you aware of whether it's raining enough or sunny enough? Is that crop, is that field, in your mind, always, even if it's not at the top of your awareness? When it's too dry, when it's too wet, when it's windy, do you worry? Do you check in?

The 14th century Spanish siddur commentator Rabbi David Abudraham, writes that we observe the *omer* in part because "the world is in danger between Pesach until Shavuot in regard to the grains and in regard to the trees." We are obligated to count these days to remember all of the hardship of the world and its vulnerability as well as our own limitations. Only in that awareness will we approach the harvest and the Divine with the intention necessary to truly be allies and partners in blessing and transformation.

Shepherds and Sentinels

Rabbi Marisa Elana James

Last fall, I was in the middle of leading a funeral and singing Psalm 23 when I suddenly began thinking about Canada geese. I began singing the line "*Adonai ro'i lo echsar*" (the divine is my shepherd, I shall lack nothing), and the image of G-d as a shepherd, guiding us to lie down in green pastures and to walk beside still water, suddenly struck me as incomplete.

On this cool, damp October day, I had driven by lots of green pastures and still waters on my way to the cemetery, and what I saw at every one was a dozen or more Canada geese, who definitely don't have a shepherd. But what they do have are sentinels.

If you watch a flock, what you'll usually see is most of the geese grazing while at least one goose stands still with its head raised high, watching. Every now and then, another goose will raise its head so the previous sentinel can take a turn grazing.

In community, humans aren't that different. In pairs or groups, we ideally watch out for each other. But I suspect that we don't often think of ourselves as shepherds or sentinels.

In Psalm 23, there's a clear divide: G-d is the guardian, and we are the ones in need of guidance, in need of comfort, in need of a divine being to prepare a table for us in the presence of our enemies. But in other texts, G-d is not the only source of strength that we can rely on.

In the book of Numbers, chapter 27, Moses asks G-d: "Let the divine source of the breath of all flesh appoint over the community someone who will go out before them and come in before them, who will lead them out and bring them in, so that G-d's community will not be like sheep that have no shepherd." Moses asks G-d to appoint humans in shepherd-like roles, similar to the roles that Moses and Aaron and Miriam played leading the Israelites out of Egypt.

Over the course of the Exodus story, there are many moments when the Israelites rely on each other to be like shepherds or sentinels. When Moses is overwhelmed by the needs of the people, his father-in-law Yitro counsels him to appoint seventy wise elders to help. The five daughters of Zelophachad stand with each other and ask to be granted their inheritance from their father's property. And a dozen Israelites are sent as scouts into the new land of Canaan to bring back reports.

Today, when we are in community and we see someone overwhelmed by impossible expectations, or someone whose rights are treated as expendable, we aren't meant to quietly wait for the divine to come with a staff and put everyone back on an ethical path. We're meant to step into a role as a shepherd or sentinel, to ask what we can do to be a good ally.

Why do I use both "shepherd" and "sentinel" here? There's an important difference: shepherds are always shepherds, but all of us are sometimes sentinels. Communities have official leaders, of course, but many of us have contexts in which we are shepherds, always watchful for what's going on, who needs support, and who might be feeling left behind.

Meanwhile, everyone in a community has times of being a sentinel. Just like in those flocks of Canada geese, in any group of people there will be a few at any given moment whose heads are up, who are paying attention to the hum of the room, who are noticing what's going on. It's partly the human habit of curiosity, but it's also partly our obligation.

There's someone in the community who just started using they/them pronouns, and another community member is repeatedly using different pronouns? If we hear that, it's our obligation to offer our support to the first person and correction to the second. There's a new member of the community who has just been introduced, and someone says to them "You don't look Jewish: how are you Jewish?" If we hear that, it's our obligation to offer our welcome and support to the first person and correction to the second.

Even when we're not shepherds, we are always sentinels, and our obligation is to help make our community a space that is safer and smarter, to help each other be more affirming, to ensure that no one is made to feel unwelcome, to notice when there's harm being done, and to make sure that the most vulnerable are being surrounded with the most love and protection.

Back in the verse from Numbers, Moses asks that the Israelite community will not be "like sheep that have no shepherd." Without a shepherd, a flock is more vulnerable to harm. Individual sheep can get lost, weaker sheep can get attacked. Without sentinels, Canada geese are also more likely to face predators. But when we commit to being good allies to each other, we're collectively stronger, and we can do for each other what G-d does in Psalm 23: we can give comfort to others by wielding their power on our behalf, we can set welcoming tables despite the presence of enemies, and we can restore each other's souls.

When the prophet Jeremiah is offering a vision of a rebuilt future to a generation that has experienced destruction, he reports that G-d offers: "I will give you shepherds according to my heart, who will shepherd you with knowledge and skill" (3:15).

Each of us is the gift that has been given to someone else. When we actively seek new knowledge and better skills to be good allies, we are acting as shepherds according to G-d's heart.

The divine is my shepherd; I shall lack nothing. My community is full of sentinels; I will not be afraid. When we walk through valleys of terrifying and difficult times, we will offer each other strength and comfort. And when enemies appear, we will set longer, more generous tables in their presence, and make sure that all who are at risk have a place at our feast.

לֹא־תְקַלֵּל חֵרֵשׁ (Lev. 19:14)/"One Shall Not Curse/Insult the Deaf:" What it Means to be an Ally to the D/deaf Community

Rabbi Darby J. Leigh

So many good, kind and well intentioned white people have been waking up over these past few years to a new awareness of the reality of living as a Black or Brown person in our deeply racist society and of the role that their own white privilege plays in perpetuating racist systems. So too hearing people might begin waking up to an understanding of their own hearing privilege in our society and come to learn how this privilege or their audism perpetuates a systemic perception of D/deaf people as "broken," defective, or somehow less than a whole, complete, full person and the subjugation or discrimination that typically results from that general perception. When seeking to be an ally to D/deaf individuals or to the D/deaf community as a whole the average hearing person would do well to keep two important texts in mind. The first text comes from the most sacred foundation of the Jewish tradition, the Torah and teaches that, "one should not insult/curse the deaf." (Leviticus 19:14) The second comes from the contemporary disability advocacy community and teaches, "nothing about us without us."

Not "insulting/cursing" the D/deaf begins by realizing that the average hearing person likely has no idea what a D/deaf person might experience as a "curse/insult." In fact, the average hearing person knows nothing of the D/deaf experience. The average hearing person does not even realize that they are hearing! The average hearing person knows nothing of the experience of living in a land where the dominant language is not your own and no matter how hard you work at it, you could never fully learn it nor have full access to it. The average hearing person knows nothing of the experience of having the way you communicate be the subject of fierce intense contentious debates, both academic and practical. The average hearing person knows nothing of realizing that your ability to access the goods, resources, and opportunities that society has to offer or to be welcomed into societal spaces depends on one's ability to "pass" for a hearing person. In fact one's speech skills and use of assistive listening devices are often the very barometer by which a D/deaf person is judged in our society and granted or denied admission to it.

Understanding what it means to not insult or curse a D/deaf person or being a true ally to a D/deaf person begins with cultivating a relationship with a D/deaf person or people. Cultivating a relationship begins with establishing communication and taking responsibility for the ways in which those in power either restrict, limit or provide access to communication. At the same time, allies must understand that addressing the challenge of communication is only a first step. Many erroneously think that "being an ally" to the D/deaf community means advocating for and creating communication access and nothing more. While communication access is an important piece of being an ally, in actuality, creating a level communication playing field is simply a basic prerequisite to being able to ultimately function as a true ally to the D/deaf community.

The D/deaf community is exceptionally diverse. It is at least as diverse as the Jewish community with a full spectrum of left to right experiences and perspectives. Within the D/deaf community some would identify as a person with a disability and others would reject that label entirely claiming it to be anathema to their experience. Nevertheless in either case the phrase "nothing about us without us" holds true. Throughout deaf history decisions about deaf people have been made by hearing people without any deaf representation or participation in the decision making process. While we might be able to "excuse" some of the more ancient examples of this due to historical context (the Talmud comes to mind) the fact that it still happens today is anywhere from ignorant to horrific and shameful.

Putting these two texts together leads to some observations and practical conclusions in the contemporary real world. The most common way that well-intentioned hearing people will attempt to be an ally to the D/deaf community is by providing an ASL interpreter or captioning at a public event. This is a wonderful gesture and absolutely essential, however, this is not "being an ally," this is simply a necessary step on the way to "becoming an ally." If providing an ASL interpreter is done without the "buy in" or "participation" of D/deaf individuals then the action runs the risk of falling short at best or coming across as offensive at worst.

I have had numerous experiences when an ASL interpreter was hired/provided with the best of intentions and yet the interpreter was not qualified for the setting/program, or stationed in a poor visibility location, or set up literally in the back of the room, or led to the dreaded, "we hired an ASL interpreter but no D/deaf people came." Hiring an ASL interpreter for an event or program ideally needs to be done in collaboration and consultation with D/deaf consumers in order to avoid some of the above potential pitfalls.

In this age of social media, digital and video communication, there is a proliferation of ASL videos online. Promoting and supporting any and all of them does not make one an ally of the D/deaf community. In fact, promoting, sharing or fawning over an ASL video that was perhaps recorded by a hearing person, who is just learning rudimentary ASL or who attempted to glean ASL signs from the Internet and is signing along to a popular "hit" song is potentially deeply offensive.

This is especially true in light of the fact that there are numerous D/deaf artists on-line who generate their own authentic ASL poetry, videos, signed songs, content and media who are often overlooked or not given due recognition. Being an ally to the D/deaf community means supporting these D/deaf artists and not hearing people who are attempting to profit in some way by borrowing or exploiting a language or tradition from a community or culture they are not personally a part of. As a recent tweet on Twitter put it, "being an ally means amplifying their voices, not to be their voice nor to raise your own."

In recent years there have also been videos circulated on line that show a deaf baby or individual having a cochlear implant activated or turned on for the first time. A cochlear implant is a surgically implanted assistive listening device. These videos appear to the uneducated as "emotional" "beautiful" or "deeply moving." I often wonder if anyone circulating such videos has ever asked a D/deaf person what seeing these videos feels like. At worst, such videos can be traumatizing to members of the D/deaf community or they can be deeply offensive in representing a rejection of culture and identity. At best they can be deeply misleading and perpetuate ignorance. Circulating such videos belies a possibly erroneous assumption about what the path forward may or may not look like for an individual with a cochlear implant or about what their long term relationship with the auditory world may actually turn out to be. Such videos fall into the realm of "disability porn" and often make hearing people feel good about themselves without having any true understanding of the deeper implications of these videos for D/deaf people.

Because the deaf community is so diverse it is impossible to come up with a pithy short explanation of what might constitute "insulting/cursing the deaf" and thus a violation of a Torah commandment. The truth is that what is insulting to one D/deaf person may not be insulting to another but one would never know which is which without a pre-existing relationship to D/deaf individuals or the community. That's where the text, "nothing about us without us" is so useful. It is a powerful reminder that in order to be successful, any attempts to be an ally to the D/deaf and to not violate Leviticus 19:14 must begin by leveling the communication playing field and then most importantly by cultivating true, deep and meaningful relationships with D/deaf individuals.

Setting a Table

Rabbi Leiah Moser

> "And he placed the table in the Tent of Meeting on the north side of the Mishkan, outside the curtain. And he set upon it the setting of bread before HaShem, just as HaShem had commanded Moses" (Shemot 40:22-23).

What does it mean to set a table for G-d? We are accustomed to thinking of the Mishkan, and later the Temple, as "G-d's house," but when we examine Moses' behavior here at the very end of Shemot, the anxious care with which he goes about setting up the Mishkan and all its furnishings is strongly evocative of a host preparing to receive an honored guest.

Earlier on in Exodus, Moses, along with Aaron and his sons and the assembled elders of Israel, become G-d's guests when they are invited to ascend Mt. Sinai. There, they behold a vision of G-d enthroned on a pavement of sapphire: "Yet Zie did not raise Hir hand against the leaders of the Israelites; they beheld G-d, and they ate and drank" (Shemot 24:11). The term here typically translated as "leaders," אצילי, occurs nowhere else in the Tanakh. Midrashically, one might be more inclined to read this word as אצלי: "close to me," or "by my side." This reading highlights the utter mystery and beauty of this moment, wherein the representatives of the people are able to enjoy a quiet meal in the very presence of the living G-d.

If in the scene on the mountain top G-d is playing host to the people, then here, in the Mishkan, we can see Israel reciprocating by playing host to G-d. In this light the Mishkan appears indeed as a house for G-d, but more specifically as a *guest house*, a sanctuary for welcoming the transcendent stranger in our midst. This way of relating to G-d as a stranger to be received with hospitality is certainly not altogether unheard of in our tradition. The most famous example involves none other than our father Abraham, who rushes to greet three strangers in the heat of the day and, of course, welcomes them with food. It is this foundational moment which is codified and ritualized in the ceremony of laying out the showbread, an act which essentially amounts to setting a table for G-d.

Consider the showbread, unlike the incense, the grain and the animal offerings, is not turned into smoke upon the altar. It remains on its table for a week or more before it is replaced with new loaves and the old ones are distributed among the priests to eat. Hence, the sole functional significance of the bread lies in the act of arranging it upon the table: an apparently simple act which manages to encapsulate a whole host of important Jewish values around the welcoming of guests and the righteous treatment of strangers, both the divine and the human. The conflation of these two categories, as in the Abraham story in which the divine messengers are initially only identified as "men," or in the idea of welcoming in holy *ushipizin* during the festival of Sukkot, where the Zohar is explicit in stating that the "portion" of the guests from above rightly belongs to the poor and the powerless who share one's table.

In a similar vein, the Babylonian Talmud (Tractate Berachot 55a) draws an explicit connection between hospitality and the atonement once associated with the sacrifices offered up on the Temple altar:

> [As for the virtue of] the one who prolongs his time at his table — perhaps a poor person will come and he will give him [something to eat]. For it is written: "The altar of wood, three cubits high," and it is written "And he said to me, 'This is the table that is before HaShem.'" (Ezekiel 41:22) It opens with the altar and finishes with the table! Rabbi Yochanan and Rabbi Elazar both say: "For as long as the Temple stood, the altar would atone for Israel. And now — a person's table atones for them."

In what sense does a person's table atone for them? This can best be understood with reference to what the Gemara says earlier: "perhaps a poor person will come and he will give him something." In other words, when it comes to atonement for our transgressions we are ultimately being judged on the basis of whether we are "making a place at the table" for someone who may have been denied a place of their own for reasons of poverty and structural inequality.

"The table" here, much like the altar it replaces in Rabbi Yochanan and Rabbi Elazar's formulation, represents not only a place of nourishment and the enactment of distributive justice through *tsedakah*, but also a point of connection. Indeed, *tsedakah* in the full sense of the term is impossible to achieve without connection, without listening to the voices of those we claim to support. The Mishkan was important for our ancestors not only as a vehicle for atonement but also as a kind of portable Sinai, a place for receiving Torah; hence its alternate title, *ohel moed*, the "tent of testimony." So too, our table of the present day, if it is to serve its role as a functional replacement for the sacrificial altar, must be for us a place of listening.

A final point: We should not fool ourselves into thinking that this act of setting a table for the stranger can ever be a *neutral* act. In Jewish tradition, justice is never a matter of remaining neutral or refusing to take sides. On the contrary, it is a matter of discerning the correct side to take and passionately upholding the rights of those who have been wronged. Perhaps unsurprisingly, in Psalm 23 we find this aspect of justice most effectively expressed in a verse which evokes the image of a set table: "You set a table for me in full view of my enemies; You anoint my head with oil; my cup overflows" (Psalms 23:5).

The divine hospitality evoked by this verse is as far as possible from a neutral act. This is why the Torah instructs us in such strong terms to *pursue* justice, to chase it down and catch it, because in an unjust world, it is the nature of justice to be elusive and difficult to hold on to.

When people lack a place at the table, this is generally because they have been *denied* a place at the table by others. If we fail to acknowledge this out of a misplaced desire to avoid conflict, then we are not living up to the Torah's call to pursue justice. It is up to us not to turn away from such conflict but to turn toward it, to pay attention to and understand the often embattled circumstances of those to whom our hearts go out in justice and, in emulation of the divine, to set for them a table "in full view" of those who would deny them a place.

Widening the Jewish Lens

Rabbi David Adelson, D. Min.

> I cry out to God from the narrow place.
> You answer me from God's wide expanse
> (Psalm 118:5).

Our view of the world, and our vision of a world transformed by justice, is limited by our own narrow perspective. But God's view is infinite. For us to imagine more compassion and more justice for all Jews and all people, we are called on to expand our field of vision, and try to see more as we imagine God might see.

Allyship can work the same way. Those of us whose identities and circumstances offer us access to power can first expand what we see and know by listening to the experiences and knowledge of those whose stories are different from our own. And then we can use our power and influence to widen the view of others with the narrative we use to describe the world and its possibility.

As a white, straight, cis male, able-bodied rabbi, I can seek to expand the range of what we mean when we say "Judaism" to include more of our story than is often taught. We move from the narrow place of an unexamined "tradition" to an expansive inclusion of more of our story. Jewish narrative, text, and tradition is so much more vast than any of us could learn in our lifetimes. What we choose to include is what we end up calling

"Judaism." When we teach and study more parts of our heritage, we bring honor to God by making known more of God's reality. That expansive version is sometimes beautiful and sometimes ugly. It makes us feel proud and it makes us feel ashamed. It feels good and it feels bad. That is okay. It is all a part of our people's story with God.

Thinking about my opportunities for allyship in my work as dean of the New York campus of Hebrew Union College-Jewish Institute of Religion, I turned to some of our students for their guidance as to what texts can serve to expand our view. I am grateful to Becky Jaye, a rabbinical student, and Kalix Jacobson, a cantorial student, for guiding me toward the following texts.

Becky directed me to a Dutch prayerbook published in 1687-8 that includes *Bracha K'shkonim avadim*, a prayer upon buying a slave (Aviva Ben-Ur, *The Centrality of Slavery: Jews in the Atlantic World*, HaSepharadi.com). Not only does our Jewish story in modernity include the horror of owning enslaved people, but in shocking and grand irony, we even ritualized their purchase in our liturgy.

When we teach and discuss such a challenging text, we tell more of the story of African-American Jews who descend from enslaved people. Some may even be the descendants of those on whose purchase this blessing was said. When we teach and discuss this text, all Jews confront what integration and acceptance in modernity has brought our people. We think of the Enlightenment as the liberation of our people. Of course, in many ways it was. But we see that the modern era also led us to participate in the historic crime of owning human beings as slaves. Those of us who benefit from white privilege must therefore reflect on the ways our integration today leads us to participate in repressive policy and individually harmful acts. It also gives us access to the power to change those policies and to act individually in ways that liberate us all. The second text, taught to me by Kalix, is Mishna Yevamot 8:6. This text includes descriptions of three categories of people, *saris*, *tumtum*, and *androginos*, who cannot be legally categorized with either males or females. These are categories of people whose diverse presentations of sexual organs make their gender categories halachically distinct from either male or female. In some cases each might be legally similar to males, or legally similar to females. The text demonstrates Judaism's identification of multiple genders. By teaching these and other texts, we demonstrate that gender identity inclusivity is not new to Judaism. By teaching these texts, we avoid the narrowness which is too often how we represent our tradition. As Kalix says, "Just read the text. It's already there."

Including more of our text and history in how we tell our story will lead to fuller inclusion of Jews of all racial and gender identities. In turn, a more fully diverse and enfranchised Jewish community will make us better able to be the allies of people of all identities in general. We can escape the narrow view that constrains us and live, fully, in God's wide expanse.

Some Jewish Principles of Allyship

Rabbi Denise L. Eger

It's hard to be an ally. Oh, some people think it's easy. Say the right words. Do the right things. Proclaim your allyship. Spout hashtags and phrases and wear the right t-shirt. But in truth, being an ally is more than words and deeper than actions. Being an ally is also a mindset. And for those of us who are Jewish, being an ally is a deep theological statement. There are Jewish principles that help us become good allies and shape our attitudes and our mindset of allyship.

At its core, allyship is an affirmation that all human beings are created in the image of the Divine, בצלם אלהים, *b'tzelem Elohim* (Gen. 1:27). This theological truth requires each person to understand that there is no "other". We are all part of a single divine fabric. While our individual circumstances might differ, ultimately we are one human family. Thus, whether it is our tribe, or national identity, our skin color, class, or our gender identity or sexual orientation that define our identities, our sense of connection is deeper and should be greater than any one aspect of who we are. In truth, many people have multiple identities and when we speak about allyship we must also be mindful that individuals are parts of many different groups and so these complexities of identity and belonging have to be honored and indeed celebrated.

The awareness needed to be an ally is also grounded in our Jewish texts. Once again, we turn to the story of Creation in the book of Genesis 3:6-7:

> When the woman saw that the fruit of the tree was good for food and pleasing to the eye, and also desirable for gaining wisdom, she took some and ate it. She also gave some to her husband, who was with her, and he ate it." And the eyes of them both were opened, and they knew that they were naked;

In this passage, long the flashpoint couched in the language of sin for violating God's command, is a moment of recognition, awakening and awareness. Upon eating the fruit of the tree of knowledge of good and evil, both Eve and Adam have an awakening. Their eyes open and they see that which they didn't previously. They become aware of their own humanity.

Part of the journey of allyship is the initial awakening and awareness of a reality of another person or group. One cannot strive to be an ally without one's eyes and one's heart opening up to the conditions of those around you. Like Eve and Adam who become aware of themselves, an ally also has a moment of awareness of their own privilege, awareness that they are in their own Garden of Eden. They have an awareness of their own humanity and other people's humanity and the relationship between them. It is that moment of awareness, tasting what may be forbidden fruit according to society at large, that opens the possibility of relating to someone else's pain, suffering and the injustices they may experience as an individual or group. As former NFL linebacker, sports commentator and facilitator of anti-racism workshops Emmanuel Acho states, "The conversations of allyship start with the self, with those tough internal monologues."[17] These internal conversations are part of the moments of awareness, and the awakenings that open our eyes and hearts. These are the first steps into allyship.

Being and becoming a good ally is more about listening than speaking. It is about solidarity and standing in the line of fire willingly, alongside those who are directly affected. A good ally does not dominate conversation. Instead they use their newly gained awareness to help change culture and sometimes even laws and codes. An ally must be in the fight to overturn oppression for the long haul. Even if laws change overnight, society and attitudes often take generations to change. Being an ally takes patience on the one hand and righteous indignation on the other not to accommodate bigotry or excuses ever.

Being an ally doesn't mean one completely understands what it is like to be oppressed. One might not know what it is like to be a person of

---

17 Acho, Emmanuel, 2020. *Uncomfortable Conversations with a Black Man.* New York: FlatIron Books, p. 183.

color, or queer, or from the working class. But when you are an ally you try to take on the struggle as your own and see the world through new and different eyes.This is the attitude adjustment we make as an ally.

Any ally tries to engage in the struggle to overturn the systemic oppression by word and deed, time and treasure. One has to recognize the privileges we are afforded. Again this consciousness, this mindset, is critical in allyship.

Some people even reject the idea of allies. The struggle against oppression of any sort must be shared because it affects the entire society.

In her article for *Marie Claire*,[18] Roxane Gay notes:

> Black people do not need allies. We need people to stand up and take on the problems borne of oppression as their own, without remove or distance.We need people to do this even if they cannot fully understand what it's like to be oppressed for their race or ethnicity, gender, sexuality, ability, class, religion, or other marker of identity.
>
> We need people to use common sense to figure out how to participate in social justice.

---

18 Gay, Roxanne, 2016. "On Making Black Lives Matter." *Marie Claire* (June 11). Available from https://www.marieclaire.com/culture/a21423/roxane-gay-philando-castile-alton-sterling/ (accessed February 5, 2021).

Our Jewish spiritual teaching around Passover teaches us this very lesson. In the Haggadah we are taught:

בכל דור ודור חיב אדם לראות את עצמו כאילו הוא יצה ממצרים.

> B'chol Dor vador chayav adam lirot et azmo k'ilu hu yatzah miMitzrayim.
>
> In every generation a person must see themselves as if they went forth from Egypt.

In other words, it happened to us then. It is happening to us now. We learn from our ancient Jewish narrative of our own people's struggles for liberation from oppression. We eat a sacred meal dedicated to recalling that liberation and vicariously re-enacting that oppression and liberation once again. The Jewish response to allyship is to use that ancient story to remind us that oppression is still happening in the world today and to do something about it! Even if we don't understand all of the problems of systemic racism or homophobia or misogyny, this passage from the Passover Haggadah reminds us that we know what oppression looks like and feels like. So be at one with those who experience oppression.

A true ally sees the world's injustices and then acts to help rectify them. It may happen in big ways, like marching in protest marches or introducing legislation to change unjust laws and lobbying to make those changes or building homes for the homeless. It also happens in small ways, during a meeting at work letting those of oppressed classes by gender, sexual orientation, ability and race have the first and last word. In other words, an ally amplifies historically oppressed voices and allows the space for those who have been silenced or sidelined to be at the center.

The Jewish mystical principle of *tzimtzum* matters. *Tzimtzum* is the idea that God contracted Godself to make space in the world for the universe. The universe exists because God withheld and made space. The same is true here. Do not take up all the space in a group, a club, a classroom, or meeting room. Withhold a bit. Make room for other voices and ideas to float freely into the decision making process, especially from people who have been marginalized or historically oppressed. It will allow for a burst of creativity and beauty and bring down more justice and equity into the world.

An ally acknowledges their own misgivings and how their own words, ideas and expressions are shaped by systems of oppression. A good ally understands that they have participated and possibly benefitted from the systems of oppression unknowingly, and is willing to re-learn and reshape their thoughts, attitudes, actions and reactions accordingly. A good ally is someone who admits their own mistakes and learns how to be gracious when criticism comes. This is the spiritual practice of *teshuva*, repentance. We can make mistakes and truly be sorry and learn to grow from our errors.

Don't make assumptions. Don't imagine or assume that you know better or more than those who are from those classes who have been oppressed. And also don't assume that every member of those classes feel exactly the same way.

Allyship is a spiritual and Jewish religious practice. Seeing people as individuals with their own experiences of the world and valuing them is a way we can express love and respect. An ally acknowledges the humanity and honors that a person can be part of a group that has historically been oppressed. An ally will stand in solidarity, including working to change and rectify the oppressive conditions. When we see each person as created in the Divine Image, the value of בצלם אלהים, *b'tzelem Elohim*, we can't help but make this a part of our religious obligation. It is truly a mitzvah, a sacred responsibility. This spiritual practice helps us to truly see another person in the fullness of their humanity.

Unlikely Brothers:
The Relationship of Moses and Aaron as a Model of Allyship

Rabba Yaffa Epstein (With thanks to Mr. Shimmy Feintuch, LCSW CASAC-G for his help and perspective in writing this piece).

We live in a world that values individuality and independence above all else. Self-sufficiency and productivity are among our highest values. We are asked to be able to find and strengthen our own voices, our own personal narratives, and our own particular identities, and bring those to bear on the world.

Yet, Jewish tradition offers us another perspective. From the very beginning of the existence of the Human being, the Torah makes a radical statement that challenges our sense of individuality:

לא טוב היות האדם לבדו : it is not good for a person to be alone (Genesis 2:18). And the solution to this "Lo Tov/Not Good" state is an "Ezer KeNegdo: A Help Mate": another human being who can help, support, and challenge us. While the original description is one of partnership, this same idea can be expanded to any partner, friend, or ally. And there is yet another model of helpmate provided in the Jewish story of allyship: that of siblings.

For most of the book of Genesis, the relationships of siblings, and in particular, of brothers is quite fraught. From the first pair of brothers in human history, Cain and Abel, which results in fratricide (!), to Isaac and Ishmael, Jacob and Esau, Joseph and his brothers, the relationship between brothers can be painful, divisive, and destructive.

Then, suddenly in the opening chapters of the book of Exodus, we are introduced to another model of siblinghood: that of Moses and Aaron.

The Allyship of Aaron to Moses

Imagine the scene: Moses, who has been separated from his family, indeed his entire nation, and has grown up in the Palace of Pharaoh, chooses his Jewish identity over his Egyptian one, and flees to Midian. There, he experiences an intimate moment of direct revelation of the Divine and is charged to become the spokesperson for the Jewish people and deliver them from slavery. Moses understandably feels unequipped and unprepared, and likely completely shocked by this Divine charge. His first response is – Who, me?! *Mi Anochi* - Who am I?

> But Moses said to G-d, "Who am I that I should go to Pharaoh and free the Israelites from Egypt?" (Exodus 3:11).

Moses's own perceived limitations, both physical and spiritual, will not allow him to undertake this awesome task. He is experiencing immense self-doubt and *he is encountering the limits of what one is capable of when they go it alone.* At first, G-d reassures Moses that G-d will be with him, but it is only later in the conversation that G-d offers another solution: Aaron, Moses's brother.

> The LORD became angry with Moses, and He said, "There is your brother Aaron the Levite. He, I know, speaks readily. Even now he is setting out to meet you, and he will be happy to see you. You shall speak to him and put the words in his mouth—I will be with you and with him as you speak, and tell both of you what to do— and he shall speak for you to the people. Thus he shall serve as your spokesman, with you playing the role of G-d to him (Exodus 4:14 – 4:16).

Interestingly, this is actually the first time that we meet Aaron! While we know earlier in the story that Moses has a sister, we were not informed of a brother until now. Further, we are introduced to him wholly in the context of being Moses's helper, support, and partner in this momentous task of confronting Pharaoh and saving the Jewish people.

While we might assume that Aaron, the older brother who has been enslaved all of this time, would feel resentment that his younger brother, who had escaped torture and slavery and had indeed run off to Midian, would be the leader of the Jewish people, G-d takes pains to assure Moses that Aaron wants this role, wants to support him, and wants to be his ally and partner in bringing redemption to the Jewish people.

This is later confirmed when the two finally meet, seemingly for the first time.

> The LORD said to Aaron, "Go to meet Moses in the wilderness." He went and met him at the mountain of G-d, and he kissed him. (Exodus 4:27).

Not only is there no resentment or jealousy on the part of Aaron, but there is actually love in his heart. Aaron here teaches us what it means to be an ally. Aaron allows himself to fill the role of helper and supporter, noticing where Moses falters and gives in to his self-doubt, and steps into exactly the spaces where Moses needs help. And, he does so with love and warmth, assuring Moses that he can do this enormous task. He causes him to understand that he is the one who can fill this role, but that Moses does not have to do so alone.

The Allyship of Moses to Aaron

Fascinatingly, in the Midrashic imagination, there is another moment where the same experience of allyship happens between these unlikely siblings. Yet this time it is Aaron who is in need of Moses's support in his moment of self doubt.

In Leviticus Chapter 9, we are told about the first sacrifices to be offered in the newly dedicated *Mishkan,* Tabernacle. Verses 7–8 read

> Then Moses said to Aaron: "Come close to the altar and sacrifice your sin offering and your burnt offering, making expiation for yourself and for the people; and sacrifice the people's offering and make expiation for them, as the LORD has commanded." Aaron came forward to the altar and slaughtered his calf of sin offering.

The Rabbis pick up on the words "Come Close to the Altar" and ask why are these words necessary? Isn't it obvious that if Aaron is offering up a sacrifice he must come close to the altar?

The Sifra, a Rabbinic Midrash on Leviticus, explains these verses as follows:

כך אמר משה לאהרן "אהרן אחי על מה נתבחרת
להיות כהן גדול אלא שתשרת לפני הקב"ה! הגס דעתך
ובא ועבד עבודתך!".

> Similarly, Moses says to Aaron: My brother, why were you chosen to become the Kohen Gadol (high-priest) as high-priest? You were chosen for this moment! Embolden yourself and perform your service! (Sifra Mechilta D' Miluim 2:8)

The Midrash is teaching us that there was a parallel moment where Aaron too experiences self-doubt. "Who am I to offer up these precious sacrifices to G-d on behalf of the Jewish people? Did I not sin with the Golden Calf? Did I not falter?" And Moses responds: "Do not give in to that self-doubt, Aaron. Indeed, you were chosen for this moment, for this service!"

Much like Aaron did for Moses at the beginning of their journey together, Moses steps in to say, with love, and with faith, "Brother, do not worry if you are worthy! Indeed, this is why you were chosen!"

Clinical social worker Shimmy Feintuch, LCSW CASAC-G, states that "Moses is showing us what a true ally is. An ally sees the pain of one who feels inadequate, unworthy of presence, unworthy of being. And more than reassuring, the ally can help remind their friend of the qualities they already possess: the parts of their person that make them up to the task."

This is indeed what we see both Aaron and Moses doing for one another. While the world calls on us to make our way as individuals, the Torah teaches us a different model. If we are living as we should, we will be asked to take on huge tasks, to bring our full and best selves to bear on the world. We will have immense moments of self-doubt, and feelings of inadequacy. In those *mi anochi/*who am I? moments, we are invited to look around for our allies. Yet, this is not enough. We must also step up and be the Moses and Aaron for one another. To see when those around us may be struggling with self-doubt, may feel overwhelmed by their own inadequacies, and say: "You do not need to do this alone, in fact you can't. I am standing next to you as you step up, and step into the roles that you were meant to fill. *Al Kach Nitbacharta*: for this you were chosen."

May we merit to be true allies for one another, and to support one another in our holy work of bettering the world.

The Ally Checklist: Seeking Justice

Rabbi Sara Paasche-Orlow

Over the past five years I have been leading an effort to make the range of older adult health care services in a large multifaceted Jewish senior care organization (from chronic care hospitals to rehab, to hospice, home care, and subsidized senior housing) welcoming and able to provide high quality care to LGBTQ older adults, and all the LGBTQ friends and family of the people in our care. This work is vital. When out of fear a person puts off seeking medical care, it can result in physical harm. Disparities in health care for LGBTQ elders persist as well as people being forced back "into the closet" to survive in residential senior care settings.[19] This is immoral.

A central component of our work is to offer culturally aligned spiritual care. Chaplains can help create a culture of care where all people are at home. To do this, we need insight into the world a person has inhabited over the course of a lifetime (e.g., what it was like for gays in the military, or a trans person in nursing school) and the adversity they might have faced, along with

---

19 Houghton, Angela. (2018). "Maintaining Dignity: A Survey of LGBT Adults Age 45 and Older," AARP. Available from https://www.aarp.org/research/topics/life/info-2018/maintaining-dignity-lgbt.html (Accessed February 16, 2021)

joyful moments of advancing equality. We need to constantly cultivate in ourselves and others curious hearts and minds. This is particularly critical and challenging as it relates to the many elders in our care who develop dementia, and the care team takes on an even bigger role in helping people maintain a sense of self and identity. Imagine what it means when dressing and presentation of self becomes the role of a caregiver.

Our work with LGBTQ elders has also helped us to work on addressing the ways racism is baked into our senior health care system. These core skills of spiritual allyship in chaplaincy also apply to how we care for and create a home for Black and Brown people including people with overlapping identities. There is even more data showing how bad health care experiences can be for LGBTQ BIPOC older people. Only when we know more about the context of people's lives, and the many hurdles and joys a person has experienced, will we be able to truly accompany them with integrity.

I have done this work by being an ally and advocate and helping advance learning and trusted relationships across our system of care. And it never stops, as there is always a next step to take to ensure that the organizational culture is changing and growing in the direction of embracing diversity, equity, inclusion, and belonging. A training session is not enough. Rainbow stickers, programming, and Pride celebrations are not enough. We have to raise up every voice, and honor the uniqueness of each person. At its core, allyship of this kind is required as a matter of social justice to insure equity. This moral requirement is addressed in traditional Jewish legal sources that guide us to recognize all the facets of damages that occur between people who do not show respect and who cause injury. These can serve as a checklist for health care and affordable housing allies.

The Talmud, Tractate Baba Kama, is an extensive treatise on personal damages. Chapter 8, entitled "When a Person Deals a Blow to a Friend," has a list of what must be considered and addressed to capture all of a person's experience so that one can be made whole again. Specifically, the Talmud (p. 83b) directs that just compensation for injury encompasses payment for: (a) physical damage, (b) pain, (c) medical cost, (d) loss of livelihood, and (e) humiliation. When we don't act as an ally, we are indeed dealing a blow to a friend, and so it is incumbent upon us to learn how to truly stand up for all who are beaten down or shut out by our social and political norms. This text, on the encompassing nature of just compensation, is a radical system for assessing the needs of the other. What might it look like to apply the ethos of this text to injury caused to LGBTQ and BIPOC people in America?

The discussion that follows in the Gemorah tries to assess how each of these elements is calculated and has many lessons that can help inform allyship if we use them as a lens into human experience. And yet, this text also contains intensely problematic attributes that require us to wrestle with them. The first category of damages is physical damage done to a person's body. But, the core Talmudic example given to exhibit the measurement of physical damage is that of a slave, i.e., the actual change in physical worth for someone sold at market. This is shocking to encounter here. The history of slavery is both long ago and quite a recent and present legacy.

We know that the legacy of the plantation overseer has not been eradicated but rather shows itself in our current police system, and throughout society. White Supremacy culture has exerted tremendous power in the open marketplace of ideas, and when we encounter slavery as an accepted reality here in the Talmud we recoil. The ally says to this text "remember this is me: not someone else." The text reminds us and leads us to remember that "my body" can also be debased and judged as chattel.

The next category of damages discussed in the Talmud relates to how pain should be measured. This is defined as how much money another person with a similar threshold for pain as the victim is willing to be paid to be made to suffer in the same way as the initial injury. This is a somewhat bizarre standard and it is unclear how they operationalized this plan. But, the goal of this method was to insist on compensation for pain with a standardized approach and from the perspective of a third party. The ally in this text is the third person in the Talmudic equation, called upon based on likeness, to feel personally another's pain and then quantify the exact cost in order to do *tikkun* (repair).

The third category for just compensation is for medical costs. The Talmud clearly did not envision the complexity of our modern health systems. The Talmud did not see access to health care as a human right. Here the ally is reminded that the cost of healthcare is simply out of reach for too many people. This includes in greater numbers LGBTQ elders, and People of Color, and must constantly work to change this. The next category of compensation for damages is loss of livelihood. The ally understands that systemic racism and stigma related to sexual and gender minorities result in loss of livelihood in comparison to white and cisgendered people and that this can be compounded over a lifetime. More LGBTQ and BIPOC seniors live in poverty and have dire needs for affordable housing than their straight and white counterparts.

And finally, the fifth Talmudic category of damages relates to humiliation. Here the Talmud measures the compensation due based on the status of the victim in relation to the one who injures them. Rashi, in his commentary on the verse explains that if a simple person is shamed, then that person's shame is great, but if an important person is shamed, their shame is greater. This classist perspective prioritizes the wealthy in a manner that is offensive. This undermines the shame that can be felt by all people regardless of class. The ally forges relationships with people who have too often been deemed less important in our social hierarchies. The ally is fierce in protecting people's honor.

This list is hugely relevant and important when working on allyship in health care. These texts are not beautiful. Indeed, they are painful. But, they provide a framework for personal and systemic review to advance allyship and equity.

Queer Advice from a Straight Rabbi[20]

Rabbi Yael Rapport

Serving the largest LGBTQ synagogue in the world, as a cis/straight rabbi, makes my position as part of CBST's clergy team a little queer. Not because my job places me deep in one of the flagship institutions of the Jewish, New York City, and LGBTQ community, but because there, I am genuinely in the minority. My heteronormativity is blessedly the exception; and being different, in this sense, makes me...queer.

This article comes from my education in this particular perspective; serving as an ally embedded within and as a leader of this ground-breaking LGBTQ Jewish community. For those of you who may, like me, be straight, gender conforming, cis rabbis, with the privileges each of these adjectives provides, I wanted to share a few thoughts on creating a leadership practice that better supports and celebrates, with pride, the opportunities we have to make Jewish communal life both a little more "queer" and a little more "average" for the LGBTQ members of our communities.

---

20 Adapted from "7 Ways Straight Jews Can Become Better LGBTQ Allies," June 15, 2018 by Mike Moskowitz and Yael Rapport. Available from: https://forward.com/scribe/403274/7-ways-straight-jews-can-become-better-lgbtq-allies/

When we look at the Jewish calendar, arguably the most festive and outwardly celebratory holiday is Purim. Costumes, masks, parties and performances frame the festivities. It has been observed that the holiest day of the year, Yom Hakippurim, alludes with its name that it is only a day "like" Purim. One interpretation is that it's very easy to feel exceptionally holy on a day that is focused exclusively on spiritual pursuits and individual introspection. But, on a day when we are eating, drinking and hiding behind our masks in a crowd, it requires more attention to feel truly holy and seen.

The Purim story of Esther's plight is one of concealed identity and the struggle to publicly acknowledge who she really is. Her name itself means "hidden" and embodies that tension. She was reluctant to reveal her innermost self, until the pain of being closeted outweighed the fear of coming out. She finds herself in circumstances of unparalleled responsibility and opportunity to save the Jewish people and she delivers. Shockingly, one of the rabbis of the Talmud also interprets her name, "Hadassah," as meaning "average."

We find this template of combining both the exceptional and the average in the story of Chana, who is struggling with infertility. When she prays for this most wanted soul, the Talmud (Brachot 31b) recontextualizes her request for "*zera anoshim*," typically translated as "male offspring," as offspring "inconspicuous among people;" or, in other words, "average."

Of all the blessings that Chana could wish for her child, why on earth would she choose for them to become average? For those of us who live our lives with our daily choices being comfortably "non-exceptional," we often don't realize what a blessing just being "inconspicuous" can be. In fact, having that level of privilege and the many blessings that come with our definition of "average" is quite exceptional.

The midrash teaches that in future times, Purim will continue to be celebrated while other holidays will become unnecessary. Perhaps, it will still resonate due to our spiritual evolution - we will embrace a new baseline of radical equality and a commonality of individuality.

So, what can we do to better hold space for the unique needs of those who are LGBTQ, while also advancing the progress of inclusivity and acceptance?

Know with certainty that in your community, whatever size or description, recognition of LGBTQ experiences matters.

Even if you *can* name LGBTQ individuals in your communities, it is still likely that someone, who you don't know, is struggling with being closeted, or trying to support a family member, and looking to you as a spiritual example for support and understanding.

There can be a large space between inviting folks and making them feel welcomed.

It's very easy to say that services are "open to all", but exceedingly difficult to make a synagogue concretely feel like a true sanctuary from the hate, discrimination, and anxiety of the wider world. What are specific, concrete ways your community could hold conversations about specialized needs?

Listen, and then listen some more.
No one's life is ever hypothetical! Allyship is an applied spiritual practice. As people's needs change, so must the resources, and we need to hear it from them, ongoing as their lives and experiences change.

When asking questions about someone's experience or relationship, check internally for the source of your curiosity.
Verbalizing the intention of being helpful and wanting to understand how can go a long way. People are more forgiving of mistakes when they see that the effort to get it right is real.

Consider positive framing to your language of inclusivity
How does it feel different to say "gender *neutral* bathroom" vs "*all* gender bathroom?" What about "you are welcome here *no matter* your gender identity/sexual orientation," vs. "you are welcome here *because* of who you are," not in spite of it?

Signage

Like the mezuzah on a doorpost shows a recognition of Jewish occupancy, Keshet's "Trans Jews Belong Here" initiative acknowledges the space as safe for folk who are trans. Bathroom access is no different. Any gendered space or ritual provides an opportunity to affirm or invalidate the identity of those present and requires a deliberate sensitivity.

Normalize speech as an act of progressive inclusivity.

- Queer universal concepts by actively choosing not to define them by their heteronormative expectation; for example, exclusively referring to "same-sex marriage." There is just marriage, whether the partners are of the same or different genders.
- Invite a person to share how they refer to themselves, and how you should refer to them, perhaps by modeling this yourself first: "Hi, I'm Rabbi Rapport and my pronouns are she/her. How shall I address you?"
- Please don't minimize this form of address by asking for a "preferred pronoun." We don't "prefer" that people use our names, our titles, and our pronouns that are often the default expectation in a heteronormative world.
- Not just when you're in doubt, but also as your default, call a person by their name

and address them directly. "I see that Yael has a hand raised: Yael, what do *you* think about this commentary?"

Know when leadership means following

Those of us who are allies have experienced many moments where feelings of urgency, empathy, and genuine good intention have impelled us to *do something* to protect the lives and rights of our LGBTQ friends. Seize that impulse, don't delay, but make your first step research and discovery.

- What are LGBTQ leading institutions and individuals advising as action? Where are LAMBDA Legal (lambdalegal.org/), the LGBTQ Center (gaycenter.org), Keshet (keshetonline.org), and CBST (cbst.org) directing their efforts and how could you support them?
- What are the essential LGBTQ institutions in your area that have been doing the work within the community, and how can you join, amplify, or underwrite their message?

Rather than jumping to an assumption of how you could be of greatest service, find out! Is a Supreme Court decision likely to affect LGBTQ rights and you want people to feel loved, protected, and seen? Marriage isn't the only thing on the table and not the only skill a rabbi has to offer: what about advance directives, second parent adoption, legal name changes? These are all deeply Jewish and deeply human civil rights that need protection: they affect more people in your community than just those who are LGBTQ.

Every society is a creation of inclusion and exclusion. Identifying a shared mission and community can help define who we are. In a world that increasingly orients by reaction and rejection of any other identity, let us elevate the most important one: we are all children of the same G-d. May we, in our regularity, embrace and honor that experience which is exceptional, and in our exceptionality, appreciate our opportunity to elevate the average.

Jerusalem Can Be a Place for Allies!

Rabbi Levi Weiman-Kelman

כשם שהטבור נתון באמצע האיש, כך ארץ ישראל נתונה באמצע העולם, וממנה יסודו של העולם יוצא. וירושלים באמצעיתה של ארץ ישראל...(תנחומא פרשת קדושים)

> Just as the navel is in the middle of each person, so Eretz Yisrael is the center of the world and the foundations of the world emerge from her. Yerushalayim is in the center of Eretz Yisrael... (Tanhuma Parshat Kedoshim)

Don't you love any sacred text that talks about our belly-buttons! What a fantastic image for the centrality of Jerusalem in Jewish consciousness! Like breathing itself, all human beings have navels. In utero it was the conduit between ourselves and our mothers, a source of nutrients. This idea has practical consequences is Jewish life. It determines how we locate ourselves physically in prayer.

העומדים בחוצה לארץ מכוונין את לבם כנגד ארץ ישראל... העומדים בארץ ישראל מכוונין את לבם כנגד ירושלם ומתפללין ...העומדים בירושלם מכוונין את לבם כנגד בית המקדש ...נמצאו עומדין בצפון פניהם לדרום בדרום פניהם לצפון במזרח פניהם למערב במערב פניהם למזרח נמצאו כל ישראל מתפללין למקום אחד. (תוספתא מסכת ברכות פרק ג' .ט"ו)

220

Those who stand to pray outside Israel direct their hearts towards Eretz Yisrael and pray... Those who stand to pray in Eretz Yisrael direct their hearts towards Yerushalayim and pray...Those who stand to pray in Yerushalayim direct their hearts towards the Temple and pray... Those who stand in the north face the south, those who stand in the south face the north, those who stand in the east face the west, those who stand in the west face the east. Thus all Jews are praying towards one place (Tosefta Brachot 3.15).

This Rabbinic text directs all Jews to face towards Jerusalem whenever we pray. That way, even if we are scattered throughout the world and praying at different times, we will be united in our focus on one particular place. It is not that all synagogues face east. My congregation in Jerusalem, Kehillat Kol HaNeshama, faces north because we are located in a southern neighborhood of Jerusalem.

The Hebrew word for direction is *kivvun* and it also gives us the word *kavanah,* or spiritual intentionality. Jewish prayer demands that we face a particular direction geographically to help us with our inner spiritual direction.

Sadly, attitudes towards Israel divide rather than unite Jews. The city of Jerusalem is characterized by conflict. There seem to be permanent tensions between the *charedim* ultra-Orthodox Jews and the rest of the population.

Especially during this time of Covid– the refusal of some (really a minority) of *charedim* to accept the guidelines about social distancing and other precautions, has led to police crackdowns on schools, weddings and massive funerals and terrifying violence and vandalism.

There is also the ongoing Palestinian-Israeli conflict that is lived out daily in a city where Jews, Christians and Muslims live right up against each other. Years ago I welcomed the highest ranking Catholic cleric, Latin Patriarch Michel Sabbach, to Kol HaNeshama for a Shabbat service. Afterwards I asked him how it compared to other synagogues that he had visited. "But this is the first time I have ever been in a synagogue," he replied. I was shocked and dismayed. Sabbach is an Israeli-born Palestinian who lives walking distance from literally hundreds of synagogues. Yet he had never been inside a synagogue or attended a Shabbat meal. We live so close to each other and yet so far.

Today is *Yom Yerushalayim:* Jerusalem Day. It commemorates the day during the Six Days War in 1967 when Israeli forces conquered (or liberated, depending on your ideology) Jordanian-controlled East Jerusalem, including the Old City and the Temple Mount. My family lived in Jerusalem in 1963 and I remember how far away the Old City felt and we climbed Mount Zion to look at the Temple Mount. As a fifteen year old in New York I vividly remember listening to the reports of the drama on WINS News and sobbing with excitement. Be careful what you wish for. A reunited Jerusalem means that much of the population lives under occupation. Today *Yom Yerushalayim* is marked by thousands of Orthodox Nationalist teenagers running through the streets of the Old City waving Israeli flags to assert our sovereignty. How can we reconcile a Jerusalem that claims to be our spiritual center and demands our devotion, to the reality of a divided city filled with warring factions?

This Midrash from Bereshit Rabbah starts at the moment after the Binding of Isaac on Mount Moriah, which according to Jewish tradition, is the Temple Mount in Jerusalem. Isaac has been spared and Abraham feels compelled to name the place.

אברהם קרא אותו יִרְאֶה , וַיִּקְרָא אַבְרָהָם שֵׁם הַמָּקוֹם הַהוּא ה'
יִרְאֶה אֲשֶׁר יֵאָמֵר הַיּוֹם בְּהַר ה' יֵרָאֶה: (בראשית כ"ב. י"ד)
שם קרא אתו שָׁלֵם , וּמַלְכִּי צֶדֶק מֶלֶךְ שָׁלֵם הוֹצִיא לֶחֶם וָיָיִן
וְהוּא כֹהֵן לְאֵל עֶלְיוֹן: (בראשית י"ד. י"ח)
אמר הקדוש ברוך הוא אם קורא אני אתו יֵרָאֶה כשם שקרא
אותו אברהם - שם, אדם צדיק, מתרעם, ואם קורא אני אותו שָׁלֵם
כשם שקרא אותו שם- אברהם, אדם צדיק ,מתרעם, אלא הריני
קוראו כמו שקראו אותו שניהם   י ר ו ש ל י ם - יֵרָאֶה-שָׁלֵם.

> Avraham called the place *Yireh* for, it was said, "It is the mount where Adonai (*yeh-rah-eh*) was seen" (Gen 22).

The midrash tells us that this conflicts with an older tradition. Shem (the son of Noah) called it *Shalem.* It says "Melchitzedek king of *Shalem* took

223

out bread and wine. He was a priest to G-d Most High *El Elyon*" (Genesis 14).

G-d is in a bind – what should the place be called?

The Holy Blessed One said: "If I call it *Yireh*, as Abraham called it, Shem, a *tzadik,* a righteous person, will be upset. If I call it *Shalem,* as Shem called it, Abraham, a *tzadik,* a righteous person, will be upset."

What can G-d do? It seems like a lose-lose situation. The midrash tells us that G-d declared Therefore I call this place as the two of them called it *Yireh-Shalem- Yeru-shalayim* Jerusalem (Genesis Rabbah 56.10).

G-d refuses to reject one name and accept the other. G-d combines both names and honors both traditions.

Jerusalem symbolizes the possibility of resolving conflicts by respecting both sides, by embracing conflicting traditions.

What a challenge to us! Are we capable of embracing others even when we come from different backgrounds and hold different views? We live in a world with such stark divisions. We feel (often rightfully) threatened by those who disagree with us. We feel that respecting others weakens us. We feel compelled to utterly reject them. This midrash offers a G-d's eye view, where the choice is not one or the other but somehow both!

As I go about my daily life in this crazy, beautiful divided city, I bump up against people who look at me and feel threatened and who terrify me. But I strive to imagine the ideal Jerusalem where we somehow embrace each other. This is the Jerusalem that I celebrate on *Yom Yerushalayim.* This is the Jerusalem we turn to in prayer.

Boaz and Ruth:
A Supporting Role

Rabba Wendy Amsellem

Ruth is desperately in need of an ally. At the start of chapter two of the Book of Ruth, she is a stranger, newly arrived in Bethlehem, without financial resources or a social network. Because she is also responsible for her older relative Naomi, she sets out in search of food and happens upon the field of Boaz. Boaz immediately notices Ruth and asks his workers who she is. A worker replies:

וַיַּעַן, הַנַּעַר הַנִּצָּב עַל-הַקּוֹצְרִים--וַיֹּאמַר: נַעֲרָה מוֹאֲבִיָּה הִיא, הַשָּׁבָה עִם-נָעֳמִי מִשְּׂדֵי מוֹאָב

> The worker in charge of the gleaners said: "She is a Moabite girl who returned with Naomi from the fields of Moav (Ruth 2.6).

From the worker's perspective, Ruth is a random refugee who is showing up to take communal resources. Boaz responds more kindly. He goes over to Ruth and invites her to continue collecting food in his field. He assures her that he has told his male workers not to harass her and he invites her to keep company with his female workers. He tells her that whenever she is thirsty, she may drink from the vessels of water provided to the workers.

Later in the chapter Boaz instructs his workers to leave extra sheaves in Ruth's path for her to collect. He invites her to join the communal lunch where she is given so much food that sated, she tucks away the leftovers for Naomi. Boaz provides for Ruth's material needs, offers her the social connections of his female workers and ensures her safety among the male gleaners. These actions make Boaz a good guy, but not necessarily a great ally. Allies not only give, but they empower.

Boaz's moment of awesome allyship occurs in the middle of the chapter. Ruth is surprised by Boaz's kindness to her and asks (Ruth 2:10) why he has extended himself given that she is a foreigner. Boaz responds:

וַיַּעַן בֹּעַז, וַיֹּאמֶר לָהּ--הֻגֵּד הֻגַּד לִי כֹּל אֲשֶׁר-עָשִׂית אֶת-חֲמוֹתֵךְ, אַחֲרֵי מוֹת אִישֵׁךְ; וַתַּעַזְבִי אָבִיךְ וְאִמֵּךְ, וְאֶרֶץ מוֹלַדְתֵּךְ, וַתֵּלְכִי, אֶל-עַם אֲשֶׁר לֹא-יָדַעַתְּ תְּמוֹל שִׁלְשׁוֹם.

Boaz said to her, I have been told what you have done for your mother-in-law, after your husband died; how you left your father and your mother and the land of your birth and went to join a people whom you did not know (Ruth 2:11)

Boaz looks at Ruth and sees her for whom she actually is. She is not a hapless hanger-on grabbing at crumbs from others' plates. Instead she is a religious hero on a noble, covenantal journey. Boaz uses the language of Abraham's original journey from his parents' home and his birthplace to the unknown land that G-d shows him (Genesis 12:1) to describe Ruth's travels. She, too, is a person on a divine mission.

Boaz adds:

יב יְשַׁלֵּם יְהוָה, פָּעֳלֵךְ; וּתְהִי מַשְׂכֻּרְתֵּךְ שְׁלֵמָה, מֵעִם יְהוָה אֱלֹהֵי יִשְׂרָאֵל, אֲשֶׁר-בָּאת, לַחֲסוֹת תַּחַת-כְּנָפָיו.

> May G-d reward you for what you have done and may you have full recompense from the G-d of Israel under whose wings you have sought shelter (Ruth 2:12).

Boaz understands that by helping Ruth he is doing G-d's work. He does not reach out to her out of a sense of pity or noblesse oblige. He understands that to be Ruth's ally empowers them both.

When we ally ourselves with others, it's critical to recognize that we are playing a supporting role in someone else's story. We have to listen closely to who they are and what their goals and dreams are and then to try to help them on their own terms.

There is a beautiful midrash in Ruth Rabbah 5:6 that makes this point succinctly. R. Yitzhak bar Maryon teaches that, while it was good that Boaz invited Ruth on that first day to a lunch of toasted barley, if he had known that his actions would be transcribed in the Book of Ruth, he would have fed her more expensive delicacies. In Boaz's mind, he was sharing his lunch with a needy stranger, which is certainly a nice thing to do. The midrash suggests though, that if Boaz knew that the story was all about Ruth and that his was a cameo appearance, he would have wanted to help her more extensively.

As allies, we show up to provide support, but we must seek to understand the other's story as they would tell it.

Allied for Torah

Rabbi Mike Moskowitz

The Talmud teaches that the Torah is only acquired *b'chabura*, within a collective (Bavli Berachot 63b). Expounding on the verse in Jeremiah 50:36, homiletically, they continue: "A sword upon the enemies of Torah scholars," a euphemism for the Torah scholars themselves, "who sit alone and study Torah." Being in a relationship with the community is a condition for learning Torah today, just as it was a prerequisite for the giving of the Torah at Mount Sinai.

Exodus 19:2 states ויחן שם ישראל נגד ההר : "Israel (singular) encamped opposite the Mountain." In Derech Eretz Zuta "G-d said since they have made themselves one encampment (*chania*), the time has come to give them my Torah." The Or Hachaim (Exodus 19:3) explains that the gathering was not a collection of separate individuals showing up together at the same time and place but was a unification of the people, coming together to complement and complete (ויחן) "Like one person with one heart" (Mechilta).

We find a similar language describing the Egyptians chasing after the Isralites (Exodus 14:10), but the order is reversed: "With one heart like one person" (Rashi). A common goal and focus can organize people, but they remain distinct and disjointed (Pachad Yitzchak). Coming together for a purpose is not the same as coming together as a person.

Allyship is often seen as a response by someone of privilege, or with resources, to the oppression or affliction of another. This is only necessary when the unity of our humanity breaks down. The more ideal model is where people are as connected to each other as they are to themselves. We wouldn't then need a commitment to "create safe spaces," or even to dismantle all unsafe spaces, because we never would have allowed them to exist at all.

Torah, when studied properly together, protects us, and preempts the need for systemic change because it gives everyone an immediate awareness of the needs and experiences of each other. It even defends against outside forces that come to challenge our peaceful coexistence. When Sennacherib came to destroy Jerusalem, King Hezekiah "inserted a sword at the entrance of the study hall and said: Anyone who does not engage in studying Torah shall be stabbed with this sword" (Bavli Sanhedrin 94b).

The word for "sword", חרב, and "ally", חבר, are the same three letters, just in a different order. Sennacherib, סנחריב, is understood as an anagram for "The prince of the sword", חרב נסי (Ben Yehyada). This is an allusion to the blessing that Esav received: "By your sword shall you live" (Genesis 27:40) and the teaching that if the voice,

קול, of Jacob is found in the study halls,[21] then the hands of Esav won't be able to hurt them (Eicha Rabbah).

The numerical value of "voice" קול and "study" למד together equal חבר "ally". Our need to learn together, as the way to acquire Torah is further alluded to in the word "chabura," collective (Ben Yehyada Brachot 63), חבורה, which is the same word as חבר, just with an additional ו and ה. The "vuv" represents the six orders of the Mishnah, and the "hey" alludes to the five books of the Torah. At the time of the giving of the Torah, allies were not needed because everything was perfect. Receiving the Torah at Mount Sinai healed the brokenness of the world. The Midrash says that there were no deficiencies, illnesses, or ailments (Mekhilta Exodus 20). All needs were provided for, and each person was whole. It was also the first time, since the Garden of Eden, that the world was safe again for G-d to come out, as G-d's self.

The blatant hatred to those whom we perceive as "other", institutionalized and mass produced by systems that oppress and dehumanize, has forced G-d back into the closet. Allyship is the recognition that we have inherited a broken world, and it is on us to fix it.

It is also a model of restorative religion. The Bal Haturim describes the two cherubs on the ark "like two chaverim engaged in the back and forth

---

21 In the verse Genesis 27:22, the word "voice" is repeated as an allusion to the necessity of having multiple voices in Torah study (B.Y. Taanit 7a).

of learning Torah" (Exodus 25:18). The Sforno adds "their wings [spread] in an upward direction, as if reflecting that they had received spiritual inspiration (from the contents of the ark) enabling them to fly".

Elevation over subjugation is the path necessary to gain entrance to sacred spaces. After humans were banished from the Garden of Eden, G-d placed the "cherubim and revolving sword, to guard the way to the tree of life" (Genesis 3:24) and continues to deny entry to those who try and limit the access of others (Teyul B'pardes p.297).

When we learn about, and with, those of a different lived experience, we expand our understanding of the Torah and fulfill its purpose in elevating humanity. We must come together, for G-d, Torah, and each other.

Subversive Wedding Liturgy: A Contribution

Rabbi Elie Kaunfer

What is the Jewish model of marriage, and how might it connect to the LGBTQ experience? Throughout the ages, the narrative basis for the blessings recited at the wedding ceremony was the first marriage: that of Adam and Eve. Indeed, of the six blessings mentioned in the Talmud (the seventh, over wine, came later), three of them are associated with the scene in which Adam marries Eve in the Garden of Eden.

But what if this model doesn't work for everyone? Of course, this has been a major challenge for those in the LGBTQ community, looking to reclaim a traditional Jewish wedding ceremony without heteronormative overtones.

To that end, and standing as an ally, I want to offer another liturgical model for the wedding ceremony that emerges in the Middle Ages. While this does not solve all the problems, it does offer another approach, which may spur further creative thinking about the wedding ceremony. And, perhaps, that is one of the ways to understand allyship: offering new pathways without fully solving all problems.

In the 14th century, recorded in a book of laws and customs from Provence, R. Aharon Ha-Kohen reports that there was an alternate form of the seven blessings recited in a special case: when a widow and widower marry. Instead of the traditional seven blessings, only one was recited:

אורחות חיים הלכות קידושין

בא"י אמ"ה בפה"ג. בא"י אמ"ה המעטירכם עטרת שמחה כעטרת בועז בבית לחם אשר ברכו אותו כל קהל ישראל והעדים העידו עליו עדות נאמנה ככתוב ויאמרו כל העם אשר בשער וגו' ["ויהי ביתך כבית פרץ" וגו'] בא"י מצליח איש ואשה.

Blessed are You YHVH, Sovereign of the Universe, who crowns you with the crown of joy, like the crown of Boaz in Bethlehem, as the whole community of Israel blessed him, and the witnesses testified true testimony about him, as it is written, "And all the people at the gate said..." "Let your house be like the house of Peretz..." (Ruth 4:11-12). Blessed are You YHVH, who makes man and woman succeed (Orhot Hayyim, Laws of Marriage, vol 2, p. 69; Kol Bo, Laws of Marriage, 75, p. 45a).

This is a striking departure from the standard blessing, which invokes the union in the Garden of Eden. Instead of Adam and Eve as the main characters of the blessing, Ruth and Boaz are the central figures. Ruth was a widow, who lost her Israelite husband named Mahlon. And according to Rabbinic tradition (B Bava Batra 91a), Boaz was a widower. In fact, the very day that Ruth returns with Naomi to Bethlehem is the day that Boaz's wife died. They encountered each other at the city gate: Ruth returning, and Boaz exiting for the burial.

235

Why is this blessing so significant? Because Ruth and Boaz could not be more different from Adam and Eve. Adam and Eve are born into the world with no past. Neither of them have previous lives that lead to their marriage; in rabbinic imagination (see B Sanhedrin 38b) their union takes place only hours after their creation! Adam and Eve's marriage is the beginning of the human race; they only look forward.

By contrast, Ruth and Boaz have a deep and winding past that precedes their union. Boaz understands himself to be too old to marry, and considers Ruth's love interest in him an act of loving kindness that goes beyond the bounds of what is expected. Ruth knows the pain of losing a spouse, as well as the disorientation of leaving her homeland and adopting a new religion. She is an outsider to the Israelite community, and might even be barred from entering that community by Torah law (see Deuteronomy 23:4). But she marries Boaz anyway, and is immediately accepted by the community, as demonstrated by the verses quoted in our blessing:

רות פרק ד

יא וַיֹּאמְרוּ כָּל־הָעָם אֲשֶׁר־בַּשַּׁעַר וְהַזְּקֵנִים עֵדִים יִתֵּן יְהֹוָה אֶת־הָאִשָּׁה הַבָּאָה אֶל־בֵּיתֶךָ כְּרָחֵל ׀ וּכְלֵאָה אֲשֶׁר בָּנוּ שְׁתֵּיהֶם אֶת־בֵּית יִשְׂרָאֵל וַעֲשֵׂה־חַיִל בְּאֶפְרָתָה וּקְרָא־שֵׁם בְּבֵית לָחֶם: יב וִיהִי בֵיתְךָ כְּבֵית פֶּרֶץ אֲשֶׁר־יָלְדָה תָמָר לִיהוּדָה מִן־ הַזֶּרַע אֲשֶׁר יִתֵּן יְהֹוָה לְךָ מִן־הַנַּעֲרָה הַזֹּאת:

All the people at the gate and the elders answered, "We are witnesses. May the LORD make the woman who is coming into

236

your house like Rachel and Leah, both of whom built up the House of Israel! Prosper in Ephrathah and perpetuate your name in Bethlehem! And may your house be like the house of Peretz whom Tamar bore to Judah—through the offspring which the LORD will give you by this young woman" (Ruth 4:11-12).

Not only is Ruth welcomed into the community of Israel by the assembled people, but also she is given the blessing to be like Rahel and Leah, the original matriarchs who literally built the Jewish people. This use of the word "build" serves as a contrast to the same word in connection with Eve, who is built from Adam's side (Genesis 2:22). Eve is passive, but Ruth is active. She is not ruled by her past, but is able to change it by striking out a new path, following Naomi to Bethlehem, and marrying Boaz.

In this union, Ruth and Boaz continue a lineage that culminates, just a few generations later, with David, the King of Israel and the harbinger of redemption. In other words, while Adam and Eve are symbols of the beginning of humanity, Ruth and Boaz are symbols of the redemption of humanity. Adam and Eve's first offspring lead to death (Cain kills Abel); but Ruth and Boaz's offspring lead to life and hope.

Note also the invocation by the assembled of Boaz's ancestor: Peretz, son of Tamar and Judah. Peretz is 10 generations before David, but his birth is also the result of a boundary-crossing union. Tamar is Judah's daughter-in-law, and she sleeps with Judah by disguising as a prostitute. Like the union of Boaz and Tamar, an Israelite and a Moabite, on its face the union of Tamar and Judah should not have led to a positive outcome; it is a forbidden union! But the Torah tells a different story; sometimes the violation of general laws are undermined by specific circumstances, and what normally is a sin leads to the redemption of the entire nation.

The model of Ruth and Boaz for marriage is not a perfect one for the LGBTQ community; on a gender level, it is still heteronormative. But the possibility of alternative narratives, encoded in new liturgical creations, is, I believe, fruitful. Ruth and Boaz offer us a couple who have a past, who have journeyed extensively before their union, and who have altered their identity significantly. In addition, they offer a vision of redemption that comes from the margins, through a union no one would have ever thought to be acceptable.

This wedding liturgy is one that did not continue in Jewish history. In the same moment of reporting this tradition, R. Aharon Ha-Kohen states that it is not the custom to say this blessing, and widows and widowers have the same standard wedding liturgy as anyone else who is to be married. But in seeing this alternative practice, perhaps we might see the seeds of alternative traditions in the wedding ceremony, and in our conception of Jewish union generally.

Reciting a Blessing on Torah Study: A Model for Wholehearted Allyship

Rabbi Atara Cohen

As allyship has become "cool" in many parts of our culture, I invite us to question the sincerity of our allyship. I periodically see bumper stickers proclaiming a driver's status as an ally, clothing brands advertising rainbow collections during Pride Month, and department stores highlighting work by designers of color. In many ways this is good: saying one cares about the essential humanity of the Other has become mainstream. However, not all, or even most, of these types of displays are examples of true allyship. Many of the people who attempt to publicly signal their allyship are not fully willing to do the work that is required to dismantle systems of oppression. The Rabbis of the Talmud were not often concerned with allyship for those who were different from them. However, the Rabbis' understanding of the sincerity necessary for important pursuits can give us language for interrogating our own important pursuit of allyship. By looking at the way the Rabbis underscored the importance of Torah study, we can see that they understood that surface-level commitments to important causes are insufficient. Just as the Rabbis critically examined their devotion to Torah, we too may examine our commitments to allyship.

To the Rabbis of the Talmud, Torah study was possibly the most important and most holy effort one could undertake. In their eyes, the designation *Talmid Chacham*, Torah Scholar, is one of the greatest honors. While they believe that one's greatness is often tied to one's depth of Torah knowledge, they are wary of the motivations that might drive a person to strive for this particular type of greatness. The Rabbis understand that there is a danger of hubris even, or especially, in this most holy of pursuits.

In Tractate *Nedarim* in the Babylonian Talmud the Rabbis explore the danger of insincerity in Torah study. An anonymous questioner asks: "And for what reason is it not common for Torah scholars to give rise to Torah scholars from among their sons?"(BT Nedarim 81a). We might have assumed the opposite: that many *Talmidei Chachamim* have children who are also Torah Scholars, but according to this questioner, that is not the case. Four Rabbis offer opinions of why this is so:

> Rav Yosef said: "This is so that they should not say the Torah is their inheritance."
>
> Rav Sheshet, son of Rav Idi, said: "This is so that they should not be presumptuous toward the community."
>
> Mar Zutra said: "Because they take advantage of their fathers' standing to lord

over the community and are punished for their conduct."

Rav Ashi said: "Because they call ordinary people donkeys." (BT Nedarim 81a)

These four answers warn of the entitlement that comes with inherited, easy, Torah access. If Torah becomes something one receives rather than something one works for, there is a danger of feeling superior to others. Torah scholarship, sacred as it is, has the potential to become the way that scholars strive to give themselves importance, rather than a force of good. Similarly, the holy endeavor of allyship has the potential to become a means to self-aggrandizement rather than a means to empower the marginalized Other. The performance of allyship might increase the revenue of a brand or might bring an individual more popularity on social media, but it often does not mean that allyship is actually happening.

The fifth answer that the Talmud offers suggests a way that we might think about true, rather than performative, action. The Talmud quotes Ravina's explanation of why Torah Scholars rarely have children who are Torah Scholars: "because they do not first recite a blessing over the Torah [before studying]"(BT Nedarim 81a).The Torah Scholar parents are punished with few Torah Scholar children because they do not recite a blessing before commencing with Torah study. The Talmud continues with a story about the dire consequences of neglecting to say this blessing. In analyzing a verse from Jeremiah, the Rabbis wonder why the Land of Israel was destroyed:

> This matter, [the question as to why the Land of Israel was destroyed] was asked of the Sages, and of the prophets, but they could not explain it. The matter remained a mystery until the Holy Blessed One explained why Eretz Yisrael was laid waste... Rav Yehuda said that Rav said: [this means] that they do not first recite a blessing over the Torah.

When the Rabbis and Prophets were stumped, G-d stepped in to answer that Israel was destroyed as a punishment for not reciting the Bracha before Torah study. While this might answer the Sages' question, we are left with many of our own: why such an extreme punishment for not reciting a blessing? What is so terrible about neglecting to say a few words?

The Maharal, a 16th century mystical thinker, asks his own question on this story: why didn't these Sages make the blessing if there were such dire consequences for not doing so? He concludes that there must be more to the blessing than simply saying the words, or they would have done so. Indeed: the intention of the blessing is that one loves G-d completely and fully for having gifted the Torah. Furthermore, "not all loves are equal, for true loves is love with one's whole heart and whole soul."[22] This is quite a high bar. We can now understand why these Sages were unable to say this blessing. For them, Torah study was a holy pursuit, but the driving force for their efforts was self-promotion rather than complete and total love.

I propose that we hold allies to a similar standard as G-d held for these Sages. If a person is not acting out of true love for the Other, if one is more concerned with one's image than the work needed to be done, then we must try harder. I do not know exactly what an allyship with one's whole heart looks like, in fact, it likely looks different for different people in different situations, but I know that it's the type of allyship that we need today.

---

22 Maharal's Tiferet Yisrael, Introduction.

Allies in Talmud

Rabbanit Ilana Fodiman-Silverman

A sage walks into a bar...

The Babylonian Talmud ends Tractate Pesachim with a story of a well-known sage at a party. While gathered at the celebration, the scholar is asked a legal detail and he doesn't know the answer. The scholar goes to the study hall to seek out and consult with others and emerges with a definitive response. The Talmudic text establishes this decision as the now established law.

From the pragmatic concern about the question posed, it is neatly resolved. However, the inclusion of this surrounding story raises some intrigue in its choice inclusion on the pages of the Talmud. Why tell the story of a scholar caught off guard at a party and unable to help? In fact, the Talmud could have recorded the law and even the deliberation without preserving in their annals the embarrassing moments that the scholar faced while unable to answer. Instead, all future generations of Talmud students are invited to re-experience this moment.

But such is not the way of the Talmud.

The Talmud as a tool in the development of the Oral tradition not only chose to preserve this single story, but over twenty-five times this formula of story is repeated in its pages. A sage is posed a question, the text declares the inability to answer and then a pivot to the study house or another scholar to resolve it. The inclusion of these stories is not meant to be a shaming of these stumped scholars, but one that attests to the nature of our oral tradition as held in human hands.

In each of these stories the language describing the "not-knowing" is identical and uses the Aramaic formulation 'לֹא הֲוָה בִּידֵיהּ': "it was not in his hands." This visual imagery is powerful. Our limited physical selves have a practical inability to hold on to everything alone. Being a scholar, who embodies Torah as a resource that people can turn to for help in answering the most difficult questions, is also about being human. Our very humanity also involves a recognition that we are not alone in this world. Humble self-awareness enables us to admit when we need help. It tempers the shame in reaching out and even developing the skills to learn where to turn to get support. This is the message that the Talmud drills home in repeating this pattern over twenty-five times in its pages.

The scholar's inability to hold the answer at the particular moment is turned into a lesson worth repeating and modelling for all of us again and again. With all of the emphasis that Jewish tradition places upon knowledge, these twenty-five repeated narratives underscore that it is not merely about knowing but about pursuing, asking, debating continuing to learn and refine ideas. These stories model a confidence and wherewithal to know that there are others that will offer support and stand by to help find answers when an individual's hands can't hold it all. It is a call to create space to bravely express our yearning and to seek out partners to find answers together.

Address Delivered at Congregation Beth Simchat Torah, New York City Shabbat, 26 October 2012

Rabbi Dan Judson

It is very special for me to be speaking at CBST 15 years after first speaking here. I want to thank Rabbis Kleinbaum and Weiss for the opportunity, and all of you who have made the internship possible. I remain deeply connected to my experience at CBST in really significant ways.

First is that I have had the great pleasure for the past five years to work at the Hebrew College Rabbinical School and one of my jobs there is to oversee the internship program, which means I get to speak with Tasha [secretarial assistant to Rabbi Kleinbaum] a few times a year about when interviews are. And just to hear Tasha's voice, I am instantly transported back here to what I am hoping is a much bigger office space now. And I also have the good fortune at Hebrew College to be the advisor to rabbinical students, some of whom you might know like Margot Meitner and Ari Lev Fornari. So I get to hear about how you all are and what things are going on here.

But beyond this great coincidence of advising your interns, I remain deeply connected to this shul and deeply grateful for the experience I had here, which impacted my rabbinate in profound ways.

So I want to tell you all a story, not really so much about when I worked here but just after I left. I did this internship in my last year of rabbinical school. And late in the year, I did what all rabbinical students do, which is, say they will never ever work in a congregation and then end up interviewing at congregations. And my then-girlfriend, now-wife, Sandy was going to Boston to do her obstetrics residency, and so I needed a job in Boston. And I interviewed with this congregation there. And they seemed lovely.

They were *mentshlikh*, they were serious about adult Jewish education, that worked for me. They were serious about observance for a Reform congregation, they were happy that I kept kosher and had a serious shabbas observance. They seemed like just solid people and it seemed like a really nice connection. Just outside of Boston, so we could live near my wife's hospital, seemed perfect.

At some point they offered me the job, and there was a period before I responded to them that one of my friends said, "Wow, Dan, I am surprised that you are going to work for them." This is not what you want to hear about your future employer. When he saw my look of puzzlement, he said, "You mean you don't know? They didn't tell you?" Again, words like "you don't know, they didn't tell you:" this is not helpful.

He told me that the reason the job at this shul was open was because they had hired a rabbi who was out. Okay, so far so good, but before she started she told them that she was pregnant. This news sent the congregation into a tizzy, and then they had a congregational meeting and decided lesbian okay, pregnant lesbian not okay, bad parental role model to be gay and having children. So they called her and reneged on their offer.

Okay then, so I was being hired by the shul that refused a lesbian rabbi. And I was not sure what to do.

I obviously thought I should ask Rabbi Kleinbaum but I wasn't quite sure how to put it. "Umm Rabbi, I know that you just invested a year of training in me, and I thought potentially I might repay that faith and trust you had in me by going to a shul that wouldn't hire a lesbian, yep, I won't let that door hit me on the way out. No problem."

So I say this in full knowledge that this does not make me look good, but I took the job. To this day, I believe a noble person would have told them to take the job and, you know, do what you do. But at that point, all other rabbi jobs were gone, I wanted to be a congregational rabbi. I just took it and hoped for the best.

I got there, and all those things I was hoping for were actually true of them. They were *mentshlikh*, they were the most serious bunch of Reform Jewish adult learners one could come across, they cared about practice, and they also, not all of them, but enough of them, wouldn't have a lesbian rabbi.

A day before Yom Kippur, the holiday where one confesses all of their wrongdoings, their sinful ways, the times when they took jobs that had dark secrets, and my phone rings. "Hello?"

"Hi Dan, Its Sharon Kleinbaum calling"

And my first thought of Rabbi Kleinbaum calling just before Yom Kippur is that the jig is up. She is on to me. Here it comes.

And she says, "I have a custom of calling the previous years' interns before the holiday to see how they are doing."

And I think, "Ah ha, she doesn't know, it's just her ritual."

And then in a moment, I hear this strange voice, and it's my voice saying to Rabbi Kleinbaum, "Umm, you know there has been something actually I have been meaning to call you about."

And there is a part of my brain that is like in those movies where someone is running in slow motion to stop something, and they are shouting, "No-o-o-o-o!" I am sure I am saying "No-oo-ooo!" but I hear myself tell Rabbi Kleinbaum about the shul and they didn't hire a lesbian, and a good person wouldn't have taken the job.

And Rabbi Kleinbaum listens, and I finish my story, and I wait. And in words that I obviously have not forgotten 15 years later, she says, "Dan, they need you. This is why we have this internship, not just so our interns can go serve GLBT [gay lesbian bisexual transgender] shuls, but so someone like you can help all those other shuls that are not safe, become safe places."

And this changed everything. I had a mission. I spent the good next ten years preaching, speaking, organizing every opportunity that came before me that we needed to be a safe community.

And my shul became that place, and we became so much more than just a safe place.

And I guess what I want to say to you all tonight is that you didn't just give me a few nice tools that I occasionally used. This internship, Rabbi Kleinbaum, and you all were directly responsible for my helping other people in profound ways.

When my shul went from being a place that didn't hire a lesbian rabbi to being one of the centers of same-sex marriage advocacy: I'll take some credit, but really it was because I had worked here.

When I performed the marriage of the vice-president of my shul and her partner (who met at my shul years earlier on a night when I had someone come do a workshop on GLBT inclusion), a few months after Sharon Kleinbaum told me they needed me; when I married them in the synagogue sanctuary on one of the first days in world history that marriage was legal, that they were having a marriage in a synagogue, and at the same synagogue which wouldn't hire a lesbian rabbi just five years before, it happened because of CBST. You helped me to help the community.

When some of the members of my shul came out to me, middle-aged folks in straight marriages who couldn't live that life any longer when the world was changing around them, hard hard cases, I had a number of them. But each, to a person, who came out to me said they felt safe coming out to me and safe coming out to the Jewish community that we had created because they knew their Jewish community was going to be supportive.

That's CBST, because Lord knows I wouldn't have any idea what in the world to do with that if l had not worked for Sharon Kleinbaum.

When I had a kid who was trans in my suburban shul, for whom most of my folks had no clue what trans even meant, my board said we all have got to get some education, we have to make them feel safe, and let this teach us something about the world we didn't know.

And I coincidentally got an email from that kid, who I had not heard from in a few years, saying they now worked in the Jewish community. That was you all.

The most significant day in my professional life was being the speaker at the rally for same-sex marriage when the legislature was having its final vote on the matter. And I was speaking in front of Boston's gay men's choir, so it was probably the only time in my life I will ever literally get to preach to the choir. But CBST was there. And when the religious leaders left that rally and walked across Boston Common to thousands of same-sex marriage supporters who were overjoyed and moved to see religious leaders on their side as opposed to the other...CBST was there. It was you helping me to make marriage a reality, make inclusion a reality and build communities that were centered on love and acceptance.

This internship is a profound thing.

My first day of work here was Irving Cooperberg's funeral, the man whom Bill Fern honored in creating the Cooperberg-Rittmaster Internship. I remember that I was just kind of a straight boy from the suburbs whose life had not been touched by AIDS, and in one day my worldview, my orientation would have to change. And I think Rabbi Kleinbaum saw me amidst all the people at the funeral before she officiated, and said to me, "Go, just go talk to people, just go and be helpful."

Lekh lekha m' artzecha umimoladetacha umi beit avicha, go forth from your native land, your birthplace and your father's house, go forth to the land that I will show you.

This week we hear the most important verse in the entire Torah. Go forth from what you knew into something different. Lord knows I am not Abraham, but when I think about it, I kind of feel like I left the familiar to come here, and then when this became familiar, I left here to a place that I was shown, to a place that needed me.

And in my trying to be a blessing to others, you all and this place have been a blessing as well.

List of Contributors

Rabbi David Adelson has served as the dean of the New York campus of Hebrew Union College-Jewish Institute of Religion since 2016 and previously served as rabbi of East End Temple in Manhattan. He holds a Doctor of Ministry degree in interfaith pastoral counseling, is a spiritual director, and is a leader in Reform movement community organizing. He is a native Brooklynite, where he lives with his spouse and two children.

Rabba Wendy Amsellem teaches Talmud and Halakha at Yeshivat Maharat and directs The Beit Midrash Program, a joint project of Maharat and Yeshivat Chovevei Torah. She also teaches regularly at Drisha, Pardes, and the Temple Emanu-El Streicker Center. Rabba Wendy received semikha from Yeshivat Maharat and is an alumna of the Drisha Scholars Circle. She has a BA in History and Literature from Harvard University.

Rabbi Guy Austrian serves as the spiritual leader of the Fort Tryon Jewish Center, an independent, traditional, egalitarian community in Washington Heights-Inwood, NYC. After a stint as a Cooperberg-Rittmaster Rabbinic Intern at CBST, he completed his studies at the Jewish Theological Seminary with rabbinic ordination and an M.A. in Liturgy.

Rabbi Rachel Barenblat is co-founder of Bayit: Building Jewish. Author of several collections of poetry, among them *Crossing the Sea* (Phoenicia, 2020), *Texts to the Holy* (Ben Yehuda, 2018), and *70 faces: Torah poems* (Phoenicia, 2011), she has blogged as the Velveteen Rabbi since 2003. In 2016 she was named as one of America's Most Inspiring Rabbis by readers of the Forward, and in 2008 *TIME* magazine named her blog one of the top 25 sites on the internet. She serves Congregation Beth Israel in North Adams, MA.

Rahel Berkovits is a senior faculty member at the Pardes Institute of Jewish Studies in Jerusalem, where she has been teaching Mishnah, Talmud and *halakha* for over twenty years. Rahel lectures widely in both Israel and abroad especially on topics concerning women and Jewish law and a Jewish sexual ethic. She is the Halakhic Editor and a writer for *Hilkhot Nashim* JOFA's Halakhic Source-guide Series, published by Koren. Rahel is a founding member of *Shirah Hadasha*, a halakhic partnership minyan, and serves on their *halakha* committee. In June 2015, Rahel received Rabbinic Ordination from Rabbis Herzl Hefter and Daniel Sperber.

Rabbi Atara Cohen is passionate about Torah which speaks to our social, intellectual, and emotional realities. She received semikha from Yeshivat Maharat in June and currently teaches Torah She'beal Peh at The Heschel Middle School.

She has studied Torah in a variety of settings, including Midreshet Nishmat, Hadar, Drisha and a BA in religion at Princeton University. During rabbinical school, Atara focused on human rights and social change through various fellowships. She served as a rabbinic intern at the Columbia-Barnard Hillel and as a Cooperberg-Rittmaster Pastoral and Educational Intern at Congregation Beit Simchat Torah. Rabbi Cohen lives in Manhattan, where she runs, knits, and experiments while cooking.

Rabbi Ayelet S. Cohen is the Senior Director of the New Israel Fund in New York. An activist, writer, and teacher, Rabbi Cohen served for a decade at Congregation Beit Simchat Torah, the world's LGBTQ synagogue serving Jews of all sexual orientations and sexual identities. Ordained at the Jewish Theological Seminary of America, she is the author of *Changing Lives, Making History: Congregation Beit Simchat Torah, The First Forty Years*, and co-editor of *Siddur B'chol L'vavcha*. Rabbi Cohen and her partner, Rabbi Marc Margolius, have five children and live in New York City.

Rabbi Menachem Creditor serves as the Pearl and Ira Meyer Scholar in Residence for UJA-Federation NY, and is the founder of Rabbis Against Gun Violence. His most recent book is "Remember and Do Not Forget." Find out more at menachemcreditor.net.

Rabbi Michelle Dardashti serves as Associate Chaplain for the Jewish Community at Brown University and Rabbi of Brown RISD Hillel. She was ordained and received a Masters in Jewish Education from the Jewish Theological Seminary and came to Brown from the congregational world, serving first as the Marshall T. Meyer Fellow at Congregation B'nai Jeshurun in Manhattan. In her eight years at Brown she has birthed a number of initiatives that think critically about allyship, activism and contemporary American Jewish positionality; among these are the Hillel Initiative on Racial Awareness and Justice and the Narrow Bridge Project.

Rabbi Denise L. Eger is the founding Sr. Rabbi of Congregation Kol Ami, West Hollywood (CA) Reform Synagogue. She is Past President of the Central Conference of American Rabbis. She served as the first openly gay or lesbian person in that position. She also was the first woman ever elected as President of the Southern California Board of Rabbis which includes Reform, Conservative, Reconstructionist and Orthodox Rabbis. She is the editor of *Mishkan Ga'avah: Where Pride Dwells, A Celebration of Jewish Life and Ritual* (CCAR Press, 2020) and an activist for LGBTQ+ rights. She is also the co-editor of *Gender and Religious Leadership: Woman Rabbis Pastors and Ministers* (Rowman and Littlefield, 2019). Eger was named as one of the 50 most influential Jews by the Jewish Daily Forward and one of the 50 most influential women rabbis. In October

2011 she was one of the Gay Icons of Equality Forum's LGBT History Month. Huffington Post named her as the #1 LGBT Clergy Person in America. Most recently recognized for her activism by the City of Los Angeles as a trailblazer, she has won numerous awards for her leadership from the Human Rights Campaign, the City of West Hollywood, the California State Senate and State Assembly. Rabbi Eger is married to Rabbi Eleanor Steinman, Associate Rabbi of Congregation Beth Shalom in Austin, TX. She has one son, Benjamin, who lives and works in Dallas You can follow her on Twitter @deniseeger or her blog "Walking Humbly. Seeking Justice. Living with Hope".

Rabba Yaffa Epstein serves as the Director of the Wexner Heritage Program at The Wexner Foundation. She formerly served as the Director of Education, North America for the Pardes Institute of Jewish Studies. She received Rabbinic Ordination from Yeshivat Maharat and holds a Law Degree from Bar-Ilan University, and has studied at the Talmud Department of Hebrew University. Yaffa taught Talmud, Jewish law, and Liturgy at Pardes for over fifteen years, and served as the Founding Director of the Beit Midrash at the Dorot Fellowship in Israel. She has lectured at Limmud Events around the globe, has written curriculum for the Global Day of Jewish Learning and has created innovative educational programming for Hillel: The Foundation for Jewish Campus Life, and Moishe House. She has participated in numerous Think Tanks on Adult Jewish Education, and has trained Rabbis and Educators from every Jewish denomination.

Kohenet Keshira haLev Fife is a Kohenet (Hebrew Priestess) and a queer Jew of Colour who delights in serving as davennatrix (shlichat tzibbur), lifespiral ceremony/ritual creatrix, liturgist, songstress, teacher and public speaker. She is Oreget Kehilah (Executive Director) of the Kohenet Hebrew Priestess Institute, founder/co-leader of Kesher Pittsburgh, Program Director of the ALEPH Kesher Fellowship, and Lead Facilitator for Keshet's GLBTQ+ Jewish Youth of Colour programming. Dual-citizens of the USA and Australia and avid travelers, she and her beloved are currently leaning into stillness and sheltering-in-peace on Osage and Haudenosaunee land, also called Pittsburgh, PA.

Rabbanit Ilana Fodiman-Silverman is Rabbanit and director of Moed, an organization based in Zichron Yaakov, Israel that draws together secular and religious Israelis in the region in shared Torah study and social action.

Rabbi Rick Jacobs is president of the Union for Reform Judaism, the largest and most diverse Jewish movement in North America. They reach more than 1.5 million people through nearly 850 congregations, fifteen overnight camps, the Reform teen youth movement NFTY, and the Religious Action Center in Washington DC. For nearly 150 years, the URJ has been at the forefront of promoting and open, inclusive, and progressive Judaism. The URJ's programs and communities inspire more and more people, from children to seniors, to explore what it means to be Jewish, to pursue justice around the world, and forge stronger ties to Israel.

Rabbi Marisa James is Director of Social Justice Programming at Congregation Beit Simchat Torah. A graduate of the Reconstructionist Rabbinical College, she previously taught English, managed a bookstore, and worked in insurance. As a teenager in Connecticut, she co-founded her high school's GSA, the second in the state. In five years living in Jerusalem, Rabbi James worked for Encounter Programs, taught in Jerusalem and Bethlehem, studied in Reform, Conservative, Orthodox, secular, and non-Jewish settings, and co-created and led the rabbinical student program for T'ruah: The Rabbinic Call for Human Rights. She and her wife live in New York City.

Rabbi Dan Judson, Ph.D., is the Dean of the Hebrew College Graduate Leadership Programs. He received his doctorate in Jewish history from Brandeis University. He is the author of *Pennies for Heaven: The History of American Synagogues and Money* which was a finalist for the National Jewish Book Award.

Rabbi Elie Kaunfer is President and CEO of the Hadar Institute. Elie has previously worked as a journalist, banker, and corporate fraud investigator. A graduate of Harvard College, he completed his doctorate in liturgy at the Jewish Theological Seminary, where he was also ordained. He also received semikha from his long-time teacher, Rav Daniel Landes. A Wexner Graduate Fellow and Dorot Fellow, Elie is the author of *Empowered Judaism: What Independent Minyanim Can Teach Us About Building Vibrant Jewish Communities.*

Rabbi Stephanie Kolin is a rabbi of Congregation Beth Elohim in Brooklyn, after having served as the Rabbi of Union Temple through the merger of these two congregations. Rabbi Kolin was ordained from the Hebrew Union College NY campus in 2006 and has, since then, served as a rabbi of Temple Israel in Boston, as the Co-Director of Just Congregations and co-founder of Reform-CA (now RAC-CA, a statewide campaign of the Reform Movement for a more just and compassionate California), and as a rabbi of Central Synagogue in Manhattan. She is equal parts rabbi and community organizer with a particular focus on superheroes. Stephanie lives in Brooklyn with her wife and their awesome daughter.

Rabbi Michael Adam Latz is husband to Michael Simon, dad to Noa and Liat, and Lead Rabbi of Shir Tikvah Congregation in Minneapolis, Minnesota since July 2009. He is the former Co-Chair of T'ruah: The Rabbinic Call for

Human Rights, a Senior Fellow at the Shalom Hartman Institute, and a pretty decent cook.

Rabbi Amichai Lau-Lavie is the Founding Spiritual Leader of Lab/Shul NYC and the creator of Storahtelling, Inc. An Israeli-born Jewish educator, writer, and performance artist, he received his rabbinical ordination from the Jewish Theological Seminary of America in 2016. Rabbi Amichai is a founding member of the Jewish Emergent Network, a member of the Global Justice Fellowship of the American Jewish World Service, serves on the Leadership Council of the New York Jewish Agenda, the Advisory Council of the International School for Peace– a Refugee Support Project in Greece, is a member of the Advisory Council for the Institute for Jewish Spirituality, and is on the faculty of the Reboot Network.

Rabbi Darby Jared Leigh is a native New Yorker who loves mountains. He is the Rabbi of Congregation Kerem Shalom in Concord MA and is committed to creating an inclusive, caring community with intellectual honesty and spiritual depth. Honored as one of *The Forward*'s "most inspiring rabbis of 2016," Rabbi Leigh is a Truth seeker, a passionate snowboarder and a former leading actor with the Tony award-winning National Theater of the Deaf. He was featured in the televised, Emmy-nominated documentary *A Place For All: Faith And Community For People With Disabilities*. Tablet

Magazine listed him as one of "15 American Rabbis You Haven't Heard Of But Should," and he has performed on stage with rock and roll bands, Jane's Addiction and Twisted Sister! Rabbi Leigh was published in Deaf Identities- Exploring New Frontiers (2019), in which he is the second author of a chapter on Religion and Deaf Identity. Rabbi Leigh also served as a consultant for the Oscar-nominated documentary *Sound and Fury* and for "Hands On," an organization that provides sign-language interpreting services for Broadway and off-Broadway productions. He worked with RitualWell.org to create online videos of ASL translations of Jewish songs and prayers. He has been a speaker for the New York City Mayor's Office for People with Disabilities, and numerous other organizations where he has taught on issues related to Deafness and disability access.

Rabbi Ellen Lippmann is the founder and Rabbi Emerita of Kolot Chayeinu/Voices of Our Lives, where she worked for 25 years with many others to build a progressive antiracist Jewish community in Brooklyn, which continues into its 28th year. Rabbi Lippmann serves on the boards of JFREJ and Integrate NYC, and is a mentor with CLI and Taproot. She was ordained in 1991 by HUC-JIR. Rabbi Lippmann and her partner are long-time Brooklyn residents and believe to be absolutely true what a Kolot Chayeinu member once said in jest: "IT DON'T GET ANY BETTER THAN BROOKLYN!"

Rabbi Dara Lithwick is passionate about building bridges between people and communities and promoting inclusion as a fundamental Jewish practice. She is an advocate for LGBTQ2+ inclusion within diverse Jewish spaces, as well as for Jewish inclusion in LGBTQ2+ spaces. When not at work as a constitutional and parliamentary affairs lawyer, Rabbi Lithwick is active as an outreach rabbi at Temple Israel Ottawa, where she helps lead services and lifecycle events, teach adult and youth programs, and engage in outreach and social action initiatives, and serves as interim rabbi at Congregation Shir Libeynu in Toronto, the longest standing LGBTQ-inclusive shul in the city. Rabbi Lithwick is also chairing a Canadian Council for Reform Judaism group to develop a Tikkun Olam strategy for Canada and is the Canadian representative to the Union for Reform Judaism's Commission on Social Action. Rabbi Lithwick and her partner love chasing their two children around Ottawa.

Rabbi Megan GoldMarche is the Rabbi at Silverstein Base Hillel in Lincoln Park and one of the Rabbis of Metro Chicago Hillel. She graduated from the University of Pennsylvania in 2006 with a B.A. in Psychology and Women's Studies. Megan was ordained by the Jewish Theological Seminary in 2014 and received an MA in Jewish Gender and Women's Studies and a certificate in Pastoral Care and Counseling. Megan and her wife Paige and daughter Brianna are thrilled to live at Base Hillel, which serves as a hub for young adults craving meaningful, welcoming, vibrant Jewish life in the best city in the world!

Rabbi Marc Margolius is a Senior Programs Director at the Institute for Jewish Spirituality, where he directs programming for lay leaders and alumni of its clergy leadership training program, as well as the Tikkun Middot Project, which integrates Jewish mindfulness with *middot* (character trait) practice. He hosts IJS's daily mindfulness meditation sessions and teaches an online program, Awareness in Action: Cultivating Character through Mindfulness and Middot. Previously, Marc served as rabbi at West End Synagogue in Manhattan. He lives in New York City with his partner, Rabbi Ayelet Cohen, Senior Regional Director for the New Israel Fund, and their children.

Rabbi David Evan Markus is North America's only pulpit rabbi simultaneously in full-time government service. In spiritual life, he is rabbi of Temple Beth El of City Island (New York, NY); Board chair and senior builder for Bayit: Building Jewish (innovation incubator); faculty in rabbinics and theology for the Academy for Jewish Religion (accredited pluralist seminary); and spiritual direction faculty for ALEPH (which he also served as Board co-chair). In secular life, David presides as judicial referee in New York Supreme Court (9th Judicial Dist.), as part of a parallel career in public service that spanned all branches and levels of government. David serves on numerous nonprofit boards, including the Center of Theological Inquiry (fueling academic theology and global public policy, adjacent to Princeton Theological Seminary). David earned double ordination as rabbi and *mashpia* from ALEPH, a Graduate Certificate in Spiritual Innovation from Columbia University's Executive MBA Program, a Juris Doctor magna cum laude from Harvard Law School, a Masters in Public Policy from Harvard University's Kennedy School of Government, and a Bachelor of Arts summa cum laude from Williams College.

Rabbi Avram Mlotek is a co-founder of Base where he serves as Director of Spiritual Life. He is the inaugural rabbi in residence at the Marlene Meyerson JCC Manhattan and author of *Why Jews Do That or 30 Questions Your Rabbi Never Answered*. *www.avrammlotek.com*.

Rabbi Ari Poster Moffic (she, her, hers) was ordained from Hebrew Union College in 2007. She graduated from Indiana University as a Religious Studies major and Baltimore Hebrew University with a master's degree in Jewish Education. Her rabbinate has been shaped by serving unaffiliated families as well as dual-faith Jewish-Christian families. She is now back to congregational work at Temple Beth-El in Northbrook, IL as their Educator. She wrote the book, *Love Remains: A Rosh Hashanah Story of Transformation*. She lives in Chicagoland with her husband, Rabbi Evan Moffic, their children and many pets.

Rabbi Leiah Moser is the rabbi of Reconstructionist Congregation Beth Israel of Ridgewood, NJ. In addition to her congregational work, she is the author of *Magical Princess Harriet,* a Jewish young adult fantasy novel whose main character is a transgender girl. She also blogs about Judaism, gender issues and neurodiversity on her website, *Dag Gadol.* In 2018 she received an Auerbach grant for her innovative experiments combining electronic music with Jewish prayer, a project which ultimately resulted in her congregation's regular "Synth-Pop Shabbat" program.

Rabbi Mike Moskowitz is the Scholar-in-Residence for Trans and Queer Jewish Studies at Congregation Beit Simchat Torah, the world's largest LGBT synagogue. He is a deeply traditional and radically progressive advocate for trans rights and a vocal ally for LGBTQ inclusivity. Rabbi Moskowitz received three Ultra-Orthodox ordinations while learning in the Mir in Jerusalem and in Beth Medrash Govoha in Lakewood, NJ. He is a David Hartman Center Fellow and the author of *Textual Activism.* His writings can be found at www.rabbimikemoskowitz.com.

Rabbi Michael Moskowitz is a rabbi at Temple Shir Shalom in West Bloomfield, Michigan. For Rabbi Mike, Judaism is about building relationships, and Temple Shir Shalom has grown through his living this mission, from 500 families when he arrived in 1995, to over 900 families today. A student of progressive values and innovation, he's game for trying new ideas and programs to celebrate Judaism and create holiness every day in our lives. From his roots in St. Louis to the Gothic playground of Duke University to even Hebrew Union College, each step of his journey has crystallized this passion. He and his wife Leslie are the proud parents of their daughter Ellie, and their twin sons, Nathan and Asher.

Maharat Rori Picker Neiss serves as the Executive Director of the Jewish Community Relations Council of St Louis. She is one of the first graduates of Yeshivat Maharat, a pioneering institution training Orthodox Jewish women to be spiritual leaders and halakhic (Jewish legal) authorities. Rori is the Chair of the Interfaith Partnership of Greater St. Louis, a David Hartman Center fellow of the Shalom Hartman Institute, and co-editor of "InterActive Faith: The Essential Interreligious Community-Building Handbook." Her passions center on Judaism, feminism, interfaith dialogue, social justice, and her three children.

Rabbi Dan Ornstein is rabbi at Congregation Ohav Shalom, a writer, and a day school Judaic Studies teacher living with his family in Albany, New York. He is the author of *Cain v. Abel: A Jewish Courtroom Drama* (Jewish Publication

Society 2020). He blogs at the *Times of Israel,* the *Jewish Forward*, and wamc.org, Northeast Public Radio.

Rabbi Sara Paasche-Orlow, BCC was ordained at JTS and serves as the Director of Spiritual Care at Hebrew SeniorLife, Boston. Hebrew SeniorLife is one of the nation's largest Jewish elder-care organizations and is Harvard's geriatric research center.

Rabbi Hara Person is the Chief Executive of the Central Conference of American Rabbis. Prior to this, she was publisher of CCAR Press and served as adjunct rabbi at Brooklyn Heights Synagogue. Since 1998, Rabbi Person has been the High Holy Day Rabbi of Congregation B'nai Olam, Fire Island Pines, NY. Rabbi Person was ordained in 1998 from HUC-JIR, after graduating from Amherst College and receiving an MA in Fine Arts from New York University/International Center of Photography. Rabbi Person lives in Brooklyn, NY, and is the mother of two wonderful adults.

Rabbi Steven Philp is currently the Rabbinic Fellow at Park Avenue Synagogue in New York City. Starting in July 2021 he will join the team at Mishkan Chicago as their new Associate Rabbi.

Rabbi Yael Rapport (she/her/hers) is an Associate Rabbi at CBST. She was ordained by the Reform Movement's HUC-JIR in 2015. Prior to her work at CBST, she served as a Chaplain Resident in the Mount Sinai Health System at Mount Sinai Beth Israel focusing on inpatient and outpatient oncology and the Gender Affirmation Surgical Unit. She is a graduate of Brandeis University with a double degree in Near Eastern and Judaic studies and Fine Arts: Art History (*summa cum laude* and Phi Beta Kappa). She has spent significant time in Israel and has studied at the University of Haifa. Rabbi Rapport has a passionate commitment to social justice: she has participated in the American Jewish World Service rabbinic student delegation to El Salvador, completed the Jewish Organizing Initiatives class for seminarians, and volunteered in the Ethiopian community in Israel and the Former Soviet Union Pesach project in Ukraine. Rabbi Rapport is a smart, thoughtful, and engaging person with great depth, both an intellectual and an artist. She is also a certified yoga teacher and a dancer.

Rabbi David M. Rosenberg has served as Coordinator of Jewish Educational Services at JCFS Chicago since 2007. He directs the JCFS Knapp Yeshiva and serves as the agency's liaison to the Orthodox Jewish community. He is co-chair of the Clergy Task Force to End Domestic Abuse in the Jewish Community of Jewish Women International. David received his BA in Russian and East European Studies from Yale University and a master's degree in Bible and rabbinical ordination from Yeshiva University. He is a graduate fellowship alumnus of the Wexner

Foundation. He loves teaching Torah and listening to music.

Rav Kohenet Taya Mâ Shere co-founded Kohenet Hebrew Priestess Institute, teaches online courses in Jewish Ancestral Healing, Embodied Presence and Pleasure as Prayer and is Assistant Professor of Organic Multireligious Ritual at Starr King School for the Ministry. She is co-author of *The Hebrew Priestess: Ancient and New Visions of Jewish Women's Spiritual Leadership* & *Siddur HaKohanot,* co-creator of the *Liberate Your Seder Haggadeck*, *Divining Pleasure* and the *Omer Oracle*, and weaves lush albums of Hebrew Goddess chant. Tune into her Jewish Ancestral Healing podcast at jewishancestralhealing.com/podcast. www.taya.ma | @tayatransforms @jewishancestralhealing.

Rabbi Rena Singer is a rabbi at Temple Sholom of Chicago and the co-founder of Modern Ritual, an Instagram that models fresh, accessible, feminist Judaism.

Rabbi Avi Strausberg is the Director of National Learning Initiatives at Hadar, and is based in Washington, DC. She received her rabbinic ordination from Hebrew College in Boston and is a Wexner Graduate Fellow. Energized by engaging creatively with Jewish text, she has written several theatre pieces inspired by the Torah and maintains a Daf Yomi haiku blog in which she writes daily Talmudic haikus. Avi is most grateful for her wife, Chana, and two children, Ori and Niv.

Rabbi Susan Talve is the founding rabbi of Central Reform Congregation, located within the city limits of St. Louis, Missouri. When other congregations were leaving the city for the suburbs, Rabbi Susan joined with a small group to be on the front line of fighting the racism and poverty plaguing the urban center. Rabbi Susan has led her congregation in promoting radical hospitality and inclusivity by developing ongoing relationships with African-American and Muslim congregations, and by fostering civil liberties for the LGBTQ+ community. Today, CRC serves as a home to generations of LGBTQ+ families and to many Jews of color of all ages.

Rabbi Lauren Tuchman is a sought after speaker, spiritual leader and educator. Ordained by The Jewish Theological Seminary in 2018, she has taught at numerous synagogues and other Jewish venues throughout North America. She was named to Jewish Week's "36 Under 36" for her innovative leadership concerning inclusion of Jews with disabilities in all aspects of Jewish life. In 2017, she delivered an ELI Talk entitled "We All Were At Sinai: The Transformative Power of Inclusive Torah." She has trained and continues to teach with Rabbi David Jaffe and the Inside Out Wisdom and Action Project, which provides a space for Jewish spiritual and contemplative practice for individuals involved in social change work. She is a participant in the Institute for Jewish Spirituality's Clergy Leadership Program. In 2020, she was honored by the Jewish Orthodox Feminist Alliance (JOFA).

Rabbi Mira Beth Wasserman, Ph.D., is on the faculty of the Reconstructionist Rabbinical College, where she teaches Rabbinic literature and culture and directs the Center for Jewish Ethics. Her book, *Jews, Gentiles, and other Animals: The Talmud after the Humanities* is an exploration of what it means to be human according to the Talmud. In connection with the Ethics Center, Mira engages in public scholarship on race, gender and Jewish ethics.

Rabbi Deborah Waxman, Ph.D., the first woman rabbi to head a Jewish congregational union and a Jewish seminary, became president of Reconstructing Judaism in 2014. She has drawn on her training as a rabbi and historian to be the Reconstructionist movement's leading voice in the public square. Under her leadership, Reconstructing Judaism has undertaken a number of major initiatives, while building even stronger relationships with affiliated congregational leadership and innovating Judaism for the 21st century. During her tenure, the organization has reimagined its rabbinical training curriculum, bolstered the movement's ties to Israel, hosted the largest convention in the movement's history, and launched an online project, Evolve, which enables substantive Jewish learning, models nuanced and respectful discussion, and serves as an incubator for ideas that can positively transform Jewish life. Rabbi Waxman is creator and host of *Hashivenu*, a popular podcast about resilience and Judaism. Rabbi Waxman has taught courses on Reconstructionist Judaism and practical rabbinics since 2002 at the rabbinical college, where she is the Aaron and Marjorie Ziegelman Presidential Professor. Waxman is a cum laude graduate of Columbia College, Columbia University, and graduated from the Reconstructionist Rabbinical College. She earned a Ph.D. in American Jewish history from Temple University.

Rabbi Levi Weiman-Kelman, a native New Yorker, is the Founding Rabbi of Kehillat Kol HaNeshama in Jerusalem and the President of Rabbis for Human Rights. He is currently translating T'Fillat Ha-Adam, the new prayer book of the Israeli Reform Movement, into English.

Rabbi Raysh Weiss, Ph.D., spiritual leader at Congregation Beth El of Bucks County, PA, holds a Ph.D. from the University of Minnesota in Comparative Literature and Cultural Studies, was ordained by the Jewish Theological Seminary, and has previously served as rabbi of the Shaar Shalom Synagogue in Halifax, Nova Scotia. Weiss is honored to be a member of Bucks POWER (Faith in Action) interfaith clergy, a former columnist for the *Canadian Jewish News*, and a political cartoonist for the *Yiddish Forward*.

Rabbi Dr. Shmuly Yanklowitz is the President and Dean of the Valley Beit Midrash, a national Jewish pluralistic adult learning & leadership center, the Founder & President of Uri L'Tzedek, a Jewish Social Justice organization, the Founder and CEO of Shamayim, a Jewish animal advocacy movement, the Founder and President of YATOM, the Jewish foster and adoption network, and the author of 21 books on Jewish ethics. *Newsweek* named Rav Shmuly one of the top 50 rabbis in America and the *Forward* named him one of the 50 most influential Jews.

Rabbi Roderick Young studied English Literature at Oxford University and Jewish studies at the Jewish Theological Seminary of America. In 1999, he was ordained at Hebrew Union College, in New York. He then became Assistant Rabbi at Congregation Beth Simchat Torah, in New York, the world's largest synagogue serving the LGBTQ+ community. In 2002 he returned to the UK and was Associate Rabbi at West London Synagogue and then Principal Rabbi of Finchley Reform Synagogue. He now lives in Norfolk, UK, and Italy with his husband Zoltan, where he writes and teaches.

Printed in Great Britain
by Amazon